'Why Don't You Just Support Arsenal?'

The Life and Times of a Spurs Supporter

Mike Daligan

Edale Press London

Published by Edale Press in 2017
Copyright © Mike Daligan, 2017
All rights reserved

ISBN 978-1-9998764-0-1

Cover Design by Paul Flowers with
additional suggestions by Gaynor Daligan

Typesetting by Divya Venkatesh

By the same author:
The Real Big Society and My Part In It
The Other Side Of The Doors
Lessons from a Chequered Life

www.mikedaligan.com

Edale Press London

Contents

Dedication

This book is dedicated to Eddy White who turned me onto Spurs in 1961; to my son, Matt, who has kept the faith; to Jem whose book provided me with insights into the inner workings of a Premier League club; to those players who made me doubt the evidence of my own eyes with their skill and audacity and to those millions of others who, no matter what team they support, share my addiction. Audere est Facere.

Preface

Just so that anyone reading this book does so without any illusions, I would like to start by saying that it is not just about football. It's about my relationship with the game, largely through my support for Spurs, but also about how the game affects those who follow it; both the highs and lows as well as the mediocre and the boring. Importantly, it's about the part that football has played in my life, through the good and not so good times. Finally, in my case, how that relationship has changed, reflected in the fact that, I watch from the comfort of a local pub these days, in contrast to when I was younger and angry with the world and that discontent could be dissipated more at the ground.

It also needs to be said that the book is largely from memory, going back to the first match that Alan Gilzean played for Spurs in December 1964 and the first one I attended at White Hart Lane. It was the start of an irrationality that I gladly accept but, deep down, don't quite understand. As I am now a grumpy old man, the anger is now expected, except that I don't enjoy being either old or grumpy. If this carries on, I will finish up as one of those who wander the streets shouting at people or engaging complete strangers in conversation, something my wife points out that I am already prone to do, much to her embarrassment. Neither are very pleasant thoughts. Maybe just going to matches and shouting abuse at the opposition, is a more attractive trait. Which begs the question, "Why is ritual abuse more socially acceptable than an old man's solitary, public anger?" There's a PhD thesis in there somewhere.

Another major point is that much of what any football supporter remembers probably comes under the banner of illusion. Your desire to believe that your team are the best, when they patently obviously aren't and that, conversely, the opposition are rubbish when they, too, are patently obviously not, is the lens through which the game is viewed and remembered. This is compounded by players whose outrageous skills can make you believe the impossible and your ever wishful mind willing the rest. Fortunately for us dreamers, some players can do just that; they can do things that take the breath away and make you doubt the evidence of your own eyes. Indeed, I know that these particular eyes have witnessed just such moments for real.

George Best and Paul Gascoigne were real people, albeit troubled geniuses. I saw them play and, boy, could they play? In other spheres, their performances would be called virtuoso. I get the impression from those I know who aren't football supporters, that a phrase that includes the words virtuoso and footballer is an oxymoron. I have to tell you that it isn't. For those of you who think that it's just a game, it is, but then Swan Lake is just a dance and The Marriage of Figaro just a musical, which they are. To those who appreciate these particular art forms, however, they are so much more than that; so it is with football. Just because the former are seen as high art and football just a game played by louts doesn't diminish the level of skill, expertise and artistry inherent in any of them. Unfortunately, prejudice, it seems, is pretty rife in all areas of society.

Most supporters, despite all the evidence to the contrary, actually believe that the team they support, usually referred to in the first person plural, as in "We played well" or "We were robbed", is the best there is. The picture is as you choose it to be and, often, not what it is or a record of what actually happened at any one moment in time. Think penalties; mainly those not given to your own team that were, in fact, 100% certainties; until, that is, you saw the action replay and, even then, you didn't quite believe it. It is that step beyond reality, but made real, that gives us hope and makes us continue to support whatever team we do until we die. It is one of the reasons we follow the game. Old Trafford isn't called the Theatre of Dreams for nothing. They, however, until they met Barcelona in the Champions League Final some years ago, at least had reason to believe that they were the best. They probably still do, despite their current position.

Perception, therefore, has much to do with our interaction with the game and, it has to be said, much else in life. Remember those people you fell madly in love with in the past before you realised what they were really like. Same with football with one notable exception; you usually fall out of love with people and move on, football allegiance isn't like that.

So this book is, as it would be for the rest of you, about my memories and my perceptions. It is the way I remember and think I saw things as I did. You will have your own, so I ask you to indulge me if you will and hope that you feel the indulgence is worthwhile. If not, well you can always support Arsenal.

Introduction

It was some years ago and I had just returned from watching Spurs on TV in my local pub. The team was going through one of its usual bad spells, only this one even worse than previous ones and my wife asked me if they'd won. "Of course not" I replied. To which her response was "Well why don't you just support Arsenal?" She had heard me admit that they played beautiful football and been successful so, for her, it was a rational response. It was, however, anathema to a Spurs supporter, even for the reasonable, intelligent, rational human being that I consider myself to be. In that moment, this book was born. Martin Jol left and Juande Ramos arrived. Spurs beat Arsenal and Chelsea along the way and, gloriously, won the Carling Cup. Then it all went pear shaped again and Juande Ramos was sacked, making him the fifth manager of the club in six years to be disposed of.

My mobile buzzed early one morning with a text that said "Wake up, you have a new manager" and, lo and behold, Harry Redknapp had arrived at White Hart Lane. I had the usual media inspired view of Harry; that is, a wheeler dealer and good at getting the best out of discarded or lower league players. Still, he was better than what Spurs had.

Unbelievably he worked miracles immediately which, at the end of the season, saw the club challenging for a place in Europe. My natural optimism returned and life, once again, looked good as did the future; just as it had done many times over the past 40 years and more. Could this be the dawning of a new era or would my hopes be dashed again? The optimist that is me genuinely believed that, in the next few years, provided that the club worked to a long term strategy, stuck with it and got some new players in, it could challenge the elite of Europe. Unfortunately, the realist that I have become keeps asking why this dawn should be any different to the others. Only time, frustration, elation and even more hair loss would tell, as it did. By the way, there's a PhD thesis in there, comparing hair loss and going grey to support for particular football clubs.

Since then, we've had Andre Vilas Boas, Tim Sherwood and, now, Mauricio Pochettino. I have to say that I've not been too enamoured with two of these; one of whom seemed to have learnt his football from books and another who was, as a manager, much as he was as a player. Yet, while hope springs eternal, over the past three years, this manager has actually brought about a real cultural change at the club. Yes, the football isn't as free flowing as I'd like it to be but Spurs are, once more, a force to be reckoned with. So, with this manager and the construction of a new 61,000 seater stadium, the future does look bright. However, as I'm prone to do, I'm getting ahead of myself already.

'Why Don't You Just Support Arsenal?'

The Life and Times of a Spurs Supporter

Beginnings

Born in South London in 1942, I neither played nor watched much football as a kid. My uncle Bill played on a Sunday morning on Blackheath with torn off book covers down the front of his socks for shin pads. I think he played full back as did his son, Mike, the cousin that I was brought up with. Both played till well past their youth and both were Millwall supporters. Indeed, I too went to see Millwall play when I was a kid until, running up the concrete terracing and not looking where I was going, I ran head first into the horizontal part of one of the metal crowd barriers. I realised then, in the appropriately named Cold Blow Lane, that standing in the cold for nearly two hours, didn't seem to me a reasonable way to pass a Saturday afternoon and, really, it wasn't. Added to this was the fact that our school, St Olave's, was a Grammar School where rugby was played; football being seen as working class, something grammar school boys weren't meant to be at that time. Even though we manifestly were.

I spent one afternoon each week at the sports ground in Townley Road playing rugby or cricket or going for cross country runs; if Dulwich Park can be called country. I remember the cold, both inside the bare hut that was our changing room and on the pitch. I also remember the single, outside, cold standpipe that we all had to queue up to wash ourselves under before we were allowed to go home. In a school that modelled itself on, and acted like, a public school (the teachers even wore black gowns); prefects, Latin, rugby, Eton fives, cold water and flagellation were prerequisites. What was it about these latter two and the English character building of those days? Somehow they were meant to toughen us up. What they didn't realise was that for many of us a lack of heating and cold water were normal at home. We went to school to get warm.

Not that those days were without their humour. Townley Road was a private thoroughfare and occasionally used by, what were called, courting couples. So when someone, running to field a ball at cricket, saw a young couple in the long grass at the edge of the sports field engaged in a different and more pleasurable leisure activity than we were, it caused a great deal of comment. One of the teachers noticed our lack of interest in the game and came over to find out what was going on. He quickly told the couple to cease their activities and leave while trying to pretend to us that they weren't doing what they obviously were. Of even more interest was finding a condom in the road which caused much hilarity and questions from us all to one of the older boys in the class who obviously knew about these things. We really were that naive in those days. The incident caused somewhat of a faux pas when I got at home that day and I threw my rugby boots under the stairs without cleaning them. My aunt asked "Aren't you going to clean those, Michael?" to which I replied, "I can't Aunt Dor, we haven't got any Durex". The word should, of course, have been dubbin and my tea was served in silence.

Later, cycling became an interest but never football. We lived over a butcher's shop on the high pavement on Old Kent Road and had little money and Arthur, the butcher's assistant and a keen cyclist, cobbled a bike together for me out of the spare parts he had. It was my passport to freedom and off I went. When we moved to the sunny uplands of Lee Green, I even got as far as Sidcup and Chislehurst Hill. Being on my own and racing against myself seemed to me a much better bet than relying on others. As you will have gathered, I am not, by nature, a team player so perhaps it was natural that team sports did not sit easily with me. Even today I enjoy the solitariness of running rather than the competitiveness inherent in team sports. The loneliness of the long distance runner never seemed to me an apt way to describe the activity.

Even the two marathons I ran in my 50's were, for me, not competitive. They were what running is always about. The enjoyment of challenging yourself, the open air and the freedom that takes place as the mind wanders in response to the metronomic gait; nature's therapy. The mental and physical effort as I push my body at the start, well worth it when the latter takes over and does the running for me. Even in the company of 30 odd thousand, when you are part of something bigger than yourself, you can still remain in your own world. The steady pace after pace that become your rhythm and helps you to complete what you set out to so that you don't feel disappointed. It's something that you do alone so that you don't let anyone else down. Like I said, I am not a natural team player.

My early memories of watching the game was on our nine inch black and white television in Manor Lane in December 1954 when Wolves were playing Honved; that plus a number of FA Cup Finals, especially the famous 1953 Matthews' Final. It was not, however, until May 1961 that my real interest in football developed. I was 19 and in the Royal Engineers in Germany, stationed in Bielefeld, and Spurs were in the Cup Final, which they would go on to win and clinch the first double of the 20th Century. Eddy White, doing his national service, was a Spurs supporter and we watched the match on a small black and white screen in the television room that the army kindly provided for its soldiers. The commentary was in German so we tuned into the British Forces Broadcasting Service so that we could listen to it in English. The fact that the radio and television commentaries didn't quite match didn't matter. I watched Spurs win. Not that I can remember much of the match.

Eddie was in the Royal Signals and worked in the office next to me in the attic of the HQ block. He was one of the last national servicemen who, out of the blue and with 6 months of their two year stint remaining, were told that they would have to do an extra six months. Whatever, Eddie talked a lot about Spurs and how they played and sufficient of it must have sunk in for me to start following their fortunes.

The Start of my Addiction

It was December 1964 and I had recently been posted from Germany to the Ministry of Defence in London. Would you believe it, I got a married quarter on the Great Cambridge Road, a 20 minute walk from White Hart Lane? For someone who doesn't take much notice of omens, perhaps this was one.

Spurs had just signed Alan Gilzean from Dundee with his debut at home to Everton on the Saturday before Xmas. It was just what I needed and off I went, leaving my wife and small daughter in our new flat, to my first real football match. If memory serves me correctly, they drew two all and Greaves scored both goals. Not unusual, as he was, and remains, the goal poacher par excellence; not bettered even today. It was the start of the partnership of the G men for Spurs and a lifetime of irrational behaviour for me. This latter is not entirely true as my behaviour up to that point had certainly not been rational and only marginally so since.

Much of the frustration with my life was alleviated, or not, watching Tottenham play, itself a frustrating experience. After that first match, I was to watch them regularly until I left the army and we moved to Stevenage in 1969. Less so between then and 1976 when I moved to Yorkshire and, largely on Sky and the computer, since my return to London in the late 1980's. Apart from the odd live game and two glorious FA Cup Finals for which I was lucky enough to get tickets, courtesy of my son, Matt; the last of these, the famous Gazza final of 1992. Spurs won both finals as they were wont to do until they played Coventry in 1987. On match days, I took up a place in the enclosure, later moving to the corner near the Paxton Road end of the ground. From someone who had hardly ever played football or watched it very much, I became an avid Tottenham fan. Doubtless, any Arsenal supporter reading this will be thinking that a lack of involvement in football is what you'd expect from a Tottenham supporter.

Spurs in those days were a force to be reckoned with, albeit somewhat sporadically. Watching them took me out of the humdrum and into another place, at least for a couple of hours on a Saturday afternoon. Given my own experiences of life as a series of high and lows, this seemed a perfect match. As any football fan will tell you, it's not just the game itself but the whole build up to the kick off that sets the scene and gets you involved. I would always set off early and, as people congregated nearer the ground and the crowd grew, I would walk faster and faster. The irrational fear that I would not get in playing out in my stomach. The urgency would only lessen when I got to the turnstile, after which it would immediately start again until I got to my usual position in the ground. Once there, with as good a view of the pitch as I could get, I could relax. As long as I made sure that someone much taller didn't squeeze in front of me between then and kick off time. There are times when territory really is important and a football match is one of them.

Those sunny August afternoons at the start of the season, when hopes were high, were something to be part of. The occasional disastrous cup defeats to opposition from the lower leagues, less so. After one particularly bad result, even though we had a party that evening, I went to bed at 9.30 and refused to get up.

The traditional battles, Arsenal, Man United, Liverpool and European evening matches were special occasions. A packed house, expectant crowd and, for those evening matches, that special sense of enclosure that is created by these conditions and the floodlight pitch within the surrounding darkness. You and 50,000 others were really in your own little bubble and, for a few hours, the world outside ceased to exist. A great many memories with some more special than others. Spurs beating Manchester United 5 – 1 after losing 5 – 1 at Old Trafford, Liverpool 2 – 1 with Jimmy Greaves scoring directly from a corner, beating Leeds 2 - 1 with Greaves, again, scoring the winner and Burnley in the cup, 4 – 3 with Gilzean getting a hat trick after being 2 – 0 down within the first 20 minutes, equalizing and, again, falling behind only to win in the end. Dave Mackay's final match at Wolves and the FA Cup semi final against Nottingham Forest at Hillsborough. Pictures of some of these are still etched in my memory despite the passage of some 50 years.

Already having a small daughter, Tracey, two years later, in July 1966, a son was born. Eight days later England played Germany in the World Cup Final. Matt obviously doesn't remember this but I lay, full length, on the sofa with the television on. He was by my side, asleep for once, and we watched England beat Germany to win the match. You can't beat father and son bonding in the old traditional ways and Matt has liked football and been a Spurs' supporter ever since.

In 1969, I left the army and my assimilation into civilian life, while essential to me, wasn't easy; a job and somewhere to live being prime considerations. Somehow, I managed it despite having a young family and a low wage. Football became less of a priority as we lived in Stevenage and had no spare money. I did, however, manage to get to the occasional game, eventually taking along that young son, who, despite the fact that he now lives in Yorkshire, carries on the family tradition. Unfortunately, it seems that his son, also Michael, is less interested in football. Indeed, there was a short while when we thought he might even become an Arsenal supporter! This would surely not have happened if Matt and

Michael's mum had stayed together and something we may both have to come to terms with one day. Fortunately, Matt now has Michael living with him so, maybe, the damage can be limited.

These days I am largely an armchair supporter. Just, I must admit, as vocal and enthused as I was when I was younger and still there, even if in spirit only. The passion still surfaces, as anyone who was in the pub when Spurs beat Arsenal on the way to the Carling Cup final a few seasons ago, will testify. Fortunately though, there are still thousands of you who do turn up rain or shine, week in and week out to support a club that should have done better. The support is there, as is the potential and the ability. Let's hope that the club can now build on that so that a new generation see the motto as more than just a Latin slogan. It will then be more than "Audere est facere"; the "dare" will have been "done".

What is it About Football?

Few are those in life who don't have some sort of interest or hobby outside of their family or work; some sort of activity that fills their leisure time. Even if is watching Eastenders. I am lucky enough, and have been for the past 35 years, to do for a living what I enjoy doing anyway, so, for me, the line between leisure and work has often been a fine one. What I am doing now, for example, writing, I enjoy and hope that it will bring me an income. Despite that, there are things I'm interested in as a purely leisure pursuit and watching Spurs is one of them. If you ask me why, I can spell out the rationale while knowing that it is not rational. Many years ago, I was in a heated discussion with a group of friends about religion and being a rationalist, I argued the rational point. One of my friends interrupted me, pointing out that you can't change someone's mind rationally when they have arrived at their views in a completely irrational way. Thus it is with football. Interestingly, I wrote a college thesis many years ago entitled, somewhat pretentiously, "The Rational Pursuit of Irrationality". It was nothing to do with watching football but it makes for an apt description of the mindset of those who follow the game. So, why should this be so?

Well, despite some evidence to the contrary, including that of my own senses, I believe that the great majority of the human race are intelligent and strive for the good and beautiful things in life. Yes, I know the reality but it helps to retain my optimism and faith in humanity, probably more so as I get older. I still believe that it is circumstances that forge people and circumstances that are not good lead people to not being good. I hope so anyway. Football, at its best, is one of those beautiful things. Played at pace, it requires thought when there is often little time to think, skill when you have little time to exercise it and perseverance when you might feel like giving up. Try thinking strategically and objectively, for example, when you have Ron Harris, Norman Hunter, Roy Keane or today's equivalent, threatening immediate physical harm closer to you than many of your nearest and dearest ever get and remember that you aren't near a toilet or wearing a nappy at the time.

The conflict between a skilful forward trying to put the ball into the net and an artistic midfielder, looking to play that forty yard pass which opens up the game, and a hard defender intent on stopping either of them, is at the centre of the battle. As is the last line of defence, the team's tame lunatic, the goalie, who can inspire a whole team with their efforts. Unfortunately, they can also destroy their hopes and undermine their confidence, secure in the knowledge that they will get the blame whatever happens.

If you remember also that it is always easier to destroy than to create, you will see that a defender should always have the edge. That probably explains why those who can score goals, or make them, are usually more highly prized than defenders. A good defender will stop the team losing; a good goal scorer can win a match in a split second. Yes, I know defenders do score goals but, unless they defend well, the team tends not to win. It is why the former are held in greater esteem than the latter and seeing that it is goals that the supporters want to see, rightly so. Think of the players that you remember: they are, almost invariably, not defenders, other than exceptional ones and, of course, goalies. The latter, the one member of the team who is allowed, and even expected, to be individualist and eccentric.

The game, at its best, is mobile, high speed, three dimensional chess played with eleven pieces on either side (Yes, I know, the Germans always win). Traditionally, the working man's weekly hour and a half's release from a life of hard work and penury. No wonder it was and remains popular. Tribalism, banter, expectation, movement, speed, skill and euphoria or disappointment, depending on the result. Always, however, the belief that winning is possible, whoever the opposition and, even when you lose, there is always the next game, next season about which you can dream and hope. I suspect that the hope is the crucial part for most of us.

Justifying being a Manchester United, Chelsea or Arsenal supporter isn't difficult. All have been top teams for as long as anyone cares to remember. But, with all due respect, how do you justify supporting Darlington, Hartlepool or Scunthorpe? The likelihood of these teams in the lower divisions winning anything is small, to say the least. Yet, to their credit, thousands turn out to support them every week. Somewhere in the region of 13.5 million people watch the premiership while another 16 million watch the football league, ie the lower divisions. That is not counting the FA and Carabao Cups and the thousands who watch non league football. Of those, a tiny proportion will see their club having any chance of winning a trophy. Yet they turn up, week in, week out, rain or shine to watch. It cannot just be about the ultimate prizes, it must be about something else. So what is it? Well, it is about football but, I would argue, it is about much else besides the game itself.

First and foremost, people identify with a particular football team. They might try to rationalise that identification but it is often after the event, post rationalisation to use the jargon. Naturally most of that identity comes from geography although not always. My local football club was Millwall but during my formative years, I didn't watch much football, so my identification certainly wasn't geographic. My cousin and his family have been a Millwall supporters all their lives; I never was. It seems, as far back as I can remember, I had thoughts about how things should be and even in the drab world that was army life, I dressed with some style. This style and attitude were reflected, I felt, in Spurs; a club that demonstrated these in the way that it played the game. Even when it lost. The supporter that I became identified with these and, by implication, demonstrated those same qualities. There again, I can be pretentious.

As the game has become global, however, that identification is not just based on geography anymore. Television has given the Premier League a worldwide audience which clubs are keen to exploit. It has also led to the overseas ownership of most of our top clubs; something that is taking the game further away from the localised support that was its heartland. Despite that, for most people, it's still about their local team. That sense of identity, that tribalism, is probably at the heart of support for any team, football or otherwise. Where globalisation will lead in the next 50 years is uncharted territory and, as I won't even be around and have enough on my plate already, perhaps best not to go there.

In the case of football and other sports, this tribalism exists within a framework of theatre and spectacle. Anyone who went to a Spurs v Manchester United game in the 60's with the gates shut 40 minutes before the kick off on a Saturday afternoon will have experienced that. The sun was shining, the pitch was a bright green, the opposition were in red, you were in dark blue and white and all around you were those with a common interest usually making a great deal of noise. The scene was set for the match that followed.

Shut into an enclosed arena with 58,000 other people, most of whom support the team that you do, on what is your home turf, waiting for your heroes to strut their stuff, is anticipation of the most intense kind. The game becomes, not just a game, but an occasion on its own, part of something bigger than itself. When those players are skilled athletes at the highest level, the game becomes art. Unfortunately, I do have to admit that I have also watched some rubbish, but, hey ho, such is life.

So, whether it has been gladiators in the arena in ancient Rome, cheerleaders at an American football match or the opening ceremony at the Olympics, humans have loved colourful spectacle. Unfortunately too, they also seem to have a proclivity for warfare, ritualised spectacle on a massive and lethal scale. Even this, too, has been watched live; witness the spectators looking down on the charge of the Light Brigade over 160 years ago. So ritualised displays, including those involving aggression, are not unusual in humanity. Go to a match, become part of the crowd, see the banners, the colours, hear the chants, the denigration of the opposition, both team and supporters, and you will see these rituals; usually good humoured, sometimes aggressive, always competitive. Just occasionally, it can spill over into actual aggression. In my experience, very seldom.

Central to these rituals is performance and the feelings and emotions this invokes. Anyone who has watched George Best, Paul Gascoigne, Lionel Messi, Pele, Bobby Moore, Dimitar Berbatov, who seemed to exhibit genuine puzzlement when he saw his team mates actually running, Jimmy Greaves, Christiano Ronaldo, Johann Cruyff, Glenn Hoddle and a host of others will know those feelings. In other spheres of activity, it might be Rudolf Nureyev, Eric Clapton, Muhammad Ali, Martina Navratilova, Paula Radcliffe, Steve Redgrave, Mo Farrar or Jessica Ennis-Hill. What they all have in common is supreme skill, expertise, hard work and an ability to dedicate much of their lives to being the best there is when most of us are just trying to get on with ours. What they also have in common is public performance before an audience gathered just to watch them demonstrating their particular skill, often in the most competitive of arenas. It is that which we go to watch, which thrills us and takes us out of the everyday. It may be bread and circuses to keep the masses happy as it has often been. Yet this love of performance and spectacle can be appreciated for itself. It has the capacity to divide or unite us and it probably always will.

For me, watching Spurs and that ability to do something that others can't is exhilarating. When that is coupled with a footballing brain that sees moves others can't even comprehend and then actually carries them out, it is beyond thrilling. Look at Pele in a World Cup match, fooling the goalie by running away from the ball knowing that the goalie would follow him thinking he had the ball at his feet when he didn't have. Outrageous genius. Unfortunately, he didn't score what would probably have been the greatest goal of them all for its sheer audacity. Then look at that beautiful picture of Bobby Moore and Pele, shirts off at the end of the match, Pele's arms almost around Bobby Moore, faces inches from one another, beaming. It encapsulates the respect and admiration that two great footballers, who not only played at the highest levels but did so in a generous spirit, had for one another. It's a photo that captures two people at the top of their game in mutual admiration of each other's work and is a moment to treasure. Tell me that that is not about skilled endeavour and achievement of the very highest order and I might suggest that you have no soul.

In considering this description, it would help if readers tried to separate what takes place on the pitch from the behaviour of a few idiot spectators off it. Just because a few hotheads behave badly (out of the many millions who watch the game) and some players cheat, does not invalidate the point. At its best football is glorious spectacle, occasion, sporting event and conflict in one. Funny, though, how the memory conveniently tends to erase the boring ones. It is, however, why football fans remain eternal optimists and, for that in this world, they should be congratulated.

Anyone who already supports a football, rugby, cricket or other club will know the feelings that this evokes. If, however, you haven't done any of these, how does it feel, that intensity, that apprehension followed by the explosion of feelings that accompany a goal; especially a winner in the last minute when you had given up hope of there ever being one? Well, in the cold light of day, I do find it difficult to describe. At the time, however, it can be indescribable. Utter elation is all I can say.

To be fair, others will have experienced that in other areas of their lives, as I have. Bearing in mind, I've been witness to the birth of my youngest daughter, run two marathons, written books and won awards. Yet that sense of seeing that winning goal has a different quality. For me, is it in the sheer emotional explosiveness of the moment. That and the fact that it is shared by thousands of others at the same time. It's a combination of occasion, identification and communality, along with an appreciation of the artistry and skill involved.

That shared emotional commitment is at the heart of support for any football team. At its best it is an uplifting of the spirit, a euphoria that transcends the everyday. At worse it can, just occasionally, will you to hope that the team lose just to show the owners that the manager is no bloody good and needs dispensing with as soon as possible. Above all, though, it's an addiction that will not let you out of its clutches and that persuades you that other things are less important, at least for that hour and a half. An academic exercise it is not.

In the most extreme cases, you and the team are one. You even talk about it in those terms. "We beat the Arsenal". Were you playing? No. Did you train the team? No. Do you work in the office? No. Did you wash the kit? No. Do you clean the offices? No. You are something that, maybe, none of those people are. You are a supporter. Without you and the thousands of others who pay their money each week, what is the club for?

Well, they're still a team but playing in front of an empty stadium with no support, no crowd, no atmosphere? Why do you think that teams are harder to beat at home than away and, in some cases, extremely so? It's the support. Think White Hart Lane as it was. Think Liverpool and the Kop, Arsenal and the North Bank, Chelsea and the Shed, United and the Stretford End. These were the heart of the club. Those hardcore supporters who sat in those areas did so as a badge of pride. Sit with them for a local derby or any big match and you can't help but be swept along with the emotion of the occasion, football lover or not. It may be chess tactically but it's also physical combat dressed up for the occasion in the club colours, another badge of pride. Why else would players kiss that badge other than to demonstrate that link with the club and the supporters? An empty gesture though it may be for many of them, they think it's important enough for them to make it. Sold to the highest bidder on wages that are beyond the dreams of most, it is unlikely that these players will even support the club they play for. These champions, like the knights of old, are paid retainers and representatives in combat, wearing the colours of clubs owned by wealthy people, usually men. It may not be royalty or the aristocracy any more but it is the new royalty, the new aristocracy. The tabloids, after all, called the Beckham's residence in Hertfordshire Beckingham Palace and the lovely Victoria must have had something in mind when she used the name Posh.

Bearing in mind that much of the Premiership is now in foreign hands, why, other than prestige and a demonstration of their wealth and power, do rich people buy football clubs? Institutions that tend not to make great profits and, in fact, often to lose money. Why, in the past, have those people supported games and other public displays? Again, probably for the same reason, prestige. Why do governments spend so much time and effort trying to bring the Olympics to their shores when the outcome is a mere two weeks of events, great displays, pageantry and massive expenditure? The same reason. It's the Roman games and knights of old writ large, as well as being, at best, awe inspiring.

So why do I, a rational human being in most of my other dealings, subscribe to this? Well it is those things I've already mentioned and the pleasure and excitement that comes with them. Interestingly, my wife, no keen football fan, was at home once after I'd recorded a match to watch. My son was with us at that time and we fast forwarded some of the action to get to the goals. Gaynor watched this and, I think, understood the action, the flow of the game and what it was about, clearly visible at high speed. Mind you, she is still no great footie fan. Neither, come to that, are my daughters. As I've said, fortunately, my son, Matt is a Spurs' supporter. Also, now, a long suffering one.

The Origins of the Game

According to Wikipedia, football is the most popular spectator sport in the world with, in the order of 3 billion people, half the total population of the planet, watching it. Quite how this is measured, I'm not sure. However, for the sake of this book, it's a figure I am prepared to accept in much the same way that we accept it when people say they are religious. It means that people watch it and are interested. Whatever, it's still an amazing figure. Given that the population of the world is estimated at just under 7 billion of which roughly half are male and half female and that football, even today, tends to be a sport which preoccupies men more, the figure of 3.3b is very impressive. It amounts to virtually the whole of the male population of the planet.

The religious analogy mentioned is actually very apposite, as religion is just as wide spread, probably more so, with just as irrational a following. At the risk of offending any readers, there is and never has been any proof in the existence of supernatural beings, yet that doesn't stop people believing in them and following rules and rituals in their worship of them. It is, I believe, called faith. Belief in the potential of your football club is much the same.

How has it come about, then, that kicking a ball within a defined set of rules between two teams of eleven people each has become the most popular sport in the world? Well it is likely that such ball games have been around for thousands of years. Not surprising really. Feet, spherical object, kick. Someone else joins in and two people play. Feet, spherical object, pass and kick. Someone else joins in and tries to stop them passing the spherical object to one another. Feet, spherical object, pass, kick and tackle. I think you get the picture; the basic essentials are there.

Among the first reports of such a game are those from China about 4,500 years ago in which balls were kicked through a net. Called tsu chu, it was played as part of the Emperor's birthday celebrations. Another game, harpastum, was played in parts of the Roman Empire and was apparently similar to an earlier Greek game called phaininda. It was a team game with varying numbers of players. More like rugby than football, it was reported to be quite violent. Comments reported from among the spectators bear a remarkable resemblance to those heard today, albeit in Latin, with "over his head" (the equivalent of "On me head, John"), "on the ground", "too short" and "pass it back" being heard. The earliest mention of a game that involved kicking a ball is contained in a verse written, probably, in the 12th century. It tells of "Four and twenty bonny boys were playing at the ball. He kicked the ball with his right foot". Not much in the way of rhyme, I have to admit.

If you had lived in medieval times, you will have been aware of a sport described as "abominable, more common, undignified and worthless than any other game, rarely ending in but with some loss, accident or disadvantage to the players themselves". You've guessed, it was football. Described as a melee without weapons, many matches were held on Shrove Tuesday. Two sides met with the captains of each deciding how many players would take part. For matches between parishes, hundreds may have done so with goals at each end several miles apart. Smaller games may have required pitches several hundred yards apart. Balls ranged from small leather ones to larger ones made of a pig's bladder filled with dried peas.

Campball, as it was called, a camp being a field, had rules which varied from locality to locality and, even, from match to match; that is if it had any at all. For much of the 14th century, the only law related to the game was that banning it. It was banned by the Mayor of London in 1314 being prohibited anywhere near the city. Edward III banned it throughout the whole country in 1331 and 1363. Games resulted in damage to property and in people being injured and, even, killed. In one particular case in 1321, William de Spalding petitioned the Pope for an indulgence because, in the course of a football match, a friend died from running into him so hard that his knife was pushed through its sheath and into the man's body. At least that was his story. Can you imagine the tabloid headline today; something that included the rhyming couplet stagger and dagger, maybe?

Even more interesting are recent reports of other animals playing the game. A wildlife organisation recently witnessed dolphins, off the Welsh coast, playing 'football' with jellyfish. This included the youngsters who copied their parents and joined in. So maybe the urge to kick a ball around for fun is much more hardwired than imagined. What is also interesting is that football, as an organised sport in this country, preceded rugby when you might have thought that throwing the ball or picking it up and running with it was the more natural option, with kicking it around being the next stage. For some reason, it wasn't. There's a PhD thesis in there too.

So what can it be that makes football so popular? I would argue that it's the beautiful game, the skill, the spectacle, the occasion and the camaraderie that I've already mentioned. It is also, I have to admit, that element of ritualised, competitive conflict. Despite the fact that we are now in the 21st Century (where did my life go?), and consider ourselves civilised (some of us) we are still a species that has evolved to protect our territory. "Fight and flight" being among the characteristics we inherit. We are, effectively, tribal and even enshrine that in our culture. "An Englishman's home is his castle" anyone? Indeed, if recent events in the political sphere are any indication, our society is becoming even more tribal, to its detriment.

In some areas of the world, we are very gradually trying to overcome that imperative but for many it is still a very evident part of their behaviour. Civilised we may consider ourselves to be but underneath beats the heart of that being who left the homeland of Africa thousands of years ago to populate the planet. If you look at the opposition next time you're at a match, you will see that some of them are still there, stripped to the waist with their winter food supply well and truly hanging over their waistband and their tribal markings displayed for all to see. They even make television appearances in the crowd scenes on Match of the Day. You will also notice that they are predominantly male. I make no further comment.

So the DNA inheritance that we carried out of Africa all those years ago, and which still determines much of our behaviour today, is played out in our sporting events and rituals. Whether it is organised religion and the idea that "our god" is better than "your god" (even though people seem to believe that it is the same one), the armed forces, the monarchy or the silly games that our politicians play. Us and them, and the demonstration that it is us and them, seems to be an important factor in almost every culture. Sad really, when there is only one human race. Despite the problems, I like being part of it but would happily get rid of the prejudices. The human race may well founder on the results of these, so let's hope that they can be dispensed with sooner rather than later. Sorry, another lecture, so back to the story.

A Brief History of the Club

There are numerous books on the history of Tottenham Hotspur Football Club so this chapter is meant as a resume to set the rest of the book in context. If you want the full details, have a good read of one of those dedicated to the club's story. A good one, if you like old books is called, aptly, "A Romance of Football, the History of Tottenham Hotspur Football Club 1882-1921". I like the romance bit because that's what it should and can be. In its preface, it describes Spurs as "one of the most popular and scientific set of exponents of the national game in the whole country". I like that bit too.

Detail being a strong point, it starts by describing the Spurs emblem, the rooster on the top of the stand. What it is made of, how tall it is, how much it cost, who made and fitted it into place and what was placed in the ball on which it stands. Some coins and souvenirs of the club's entry into the old First Division in 1909, if you are curious. It didn't, however, describe the weather on the day it was erected or what the workmen had for lunch. Still you can't have everything. Fascinating stuff, though, for the train spotters among you and for many ardent fans. I particularly like the statement in the book that " Like the little brook that ripples its way among the hills grows into a sturdy stream, flows on through smiling fields and desert rocks and finally expands into a mighty river, so has been the career of the mighty Tottenham club".

The club that is now known at Tottenham Hotspur was formed in 1882 by a group of boys from St John's Presbyterian School and Hotspur Cricket Club. It was first called Hotspur Football Club after Sir Henry Percy, who was the eldest son of the first Earl of Northumberland in the 14th century and went by the name "Harry Hotspur". Moreover, he was renowned for being fearless. You get the picture. Incidentally, is seems that Spurs is the only club to be named after a character in a play written by Shakespeare.

According to the book, the club arose out of the rivalry of various groups of young men who played football in the area. These included the "Cads" of the High Road, "Barker's Bulldogs", pupils from Lancastrian School, the "Northumberland Pups" who lived in Northumberland Park, and "Simmonds' Greyhounds" from Park Lane schools. Although there may well have been rivalry and violence, "Gangs of New York" it probably was not. Out of this came an approach, by some of the lads, to John Ripsher, a local dignitary. A meeting was organised and, in August 1883, a football club was duly created. The first match that was recorded (in the pages of the "Weekly Herald") was on 6 October 1883 against Brownlow Rovers which Spurs won 9-0. An auspicious start.

John Ripsher became the club's first president being described, in a history dated 1908, as the club's "real father and founder". He reorganised the club before leaving, in 1894, with Spurs playing in the Southern Alliance League and with their own ground at Northumberland Park. John later moved to Dover where he died in the local workhouse on September 24, 1907. He was buried in a pauper's grave without a headstone. 100 years later, on the club's 125th anniversary, thanks to Peter Lupton, a semi retired teacher from Liverpool, his grave was identified and a headstone placed on it to mark his contribution to the club. Nice one, Peter.

By 1898, Spurs had become a professional club playing in the Southern League in front of 14,000 spectators. It seems that, soon after, they acquired a piece of land next to the White Hart and built a new ground. The first match in this was against Notts County, the world's oldest football league club, in 1899.

Spurs went on to win promotion to the league in 1908 where they struggled somewhat until football was suspended on the outbreak of the First World War. On the resumption of the league programme, the club won promotion from the Second Division in 1920 and the FA Cup the following year. In doing so, they became the only non league team to do so since they last won it in 1901, when they beat Sheffield United and started somewhat of a trend in winning the Cup in seasons beginning with a 1. They were relegated in 1928 staying in the Second Division until 1933. They once again won promotion only to be relegated again in 1935. With the outbreak of the Second World War in 1939 and the suspension of league football again, they were to remain in the Second Division until 1950.

It is probably fair to say that, following the appointment of Arthur Rowe as manager in 1949, the same year that Bill Shankly retired as a player, the modern Spurs era began. Arthur Rowe established "push and run" as Spurs' style. This involves passing the ball to a team mate and running past the opposing defender to receive the return pass. It was so effective that the club was again promoted in 1950 going on to win the old First Division Championship the following season. Bill Nicholson played at right half and the team that Spurs pipped for the title was Manchester United, managed by one Matt Busby. Apart from one season, they have been in the top division ever since. That team broke up and, again, the club went through a bad spell until, in 1958, Bill was appointed as manager. They walloped Everton 10-4 on his first match in charge and the rest, as they say, is history.

Despite, however, a continuation of some level of success in the 1970's and 80's and a somewhat lower level in the

1990's, those times have not been repeated. It is about time that they were so that this glorious history continues, to become a glorious present. Historians can then themselves write of our present in which the beautiful game was beautifully played by a team with a proud tradition of such football. Danny Blanchflower's dictum about glory and style will once again be spoken of at White Hart Lane. The example will, again, have been set. Audere est facere indeed.

Why Spurs?

Over 50 years have gone by since the first time I went to White Hart Lane and, for much of that time, I believed that next season would be better and that Spurs would win something important. Was I deluded? Well, maybe was I for much of that time but, it would seem, maybe not any longer; and you wouldn't be a Spurs' supporters without that inbuilt "maybe" there. Despite all the good that is now happening, it's hard to shake of the pessimism that lurks beneath the surface. Still, I'm in good company with the thousands of others who believe that "Audere est facere" or whatever Latin motto their particular club has chosen to describe its ethos. There's a PhD in there researching why mottoes are usually in Latin and why they sound more important because of that.

During that time and until recently, I have seen Spurs win, lose and draw (the only alternatives on offer). Sometimes gloriously, sometimes not too well, but always in a manner that I tried to identify as Tottenham's. It's summed up in the quotation from the immortal Danny Blanchflower, "The great fallacy is that the game is first and last about winning. It is nothing of the kind. The game is about glory. It is about doing things in style and with a flourish, about going out and beating the other lot, not waiting for them to die of boredom."

It is, just occasionally, about realising that life can be different and that dreams can become reality; something well and truly demonstrated by Leicester City in 2015/16. Yet, although winning is important, it has to be with some style. And yes, you can have the best of all worlds; winning doesn't have to be at the expense of what you believe in. There will always be those of a more pragmatic bent who may clock up a record of success. What they won't leave behind is that special legacy in which respect is allied to affection. That's the reason that some team are loved and others not so. Think Leeds United in the 70's. They did play some lovely football and were successful, but winning at all costs was the name of the game for them. That team is still a byword for "professionalism" or getting away with it and that has eclipsed the legacy of their football, superb though it was at times.

I've been lucky enough, over much of past 37 years to, either have been able to turn dreams into reality or to have been paid for what I've enjoyed doing, often both. Unfortunately, many people work to earn a wage just to enable them to live and to do, in their spare time, what they'd really like to do. Professional footballers, however, not only enjoy what they do for a living but get extremely well paid in the process. I too have been somewhat fortunate in that respect, other than the earning good money bit. My dream worlds have been the charities and community projects I have saved or created. Many of these have been that little bit of wonderland for those involved and I have been lucky enough to create mine on a number of occasions. I like to think that life could be like that all the time. Why not? After all you only have one life, so try to enjoy it. It ain't no dress rehearsal as, I think, Malcolm Allison said. But, I digress, so back to football.

The game, I would argue is about means and not just ends, method and not results. Indeed I would go further and argue that the boring teams are only able to get away with it because of those that try to play the game in the way that it should be played. After all, if everyone played boring football, gates would eventually drop. Even the most ardent supporters would probably get fed up and certainly there would be fewer new ones.

Indeed, a Chelsea supporter recently admitted to me that, even those Chelsea fans he knew got bored with what they saw as Jose Mourinho's "results before artistry" philosophy, although he didn't put it that subtlety as that. Mind you they did re-employ him, with some success, only to sack him again when they'd had enough. Yet, I'm told that, on a personal basis, he can be quite amenable. There's a PhD thesis in there too.

The teams you admire, despite the fact that they're the opposition, thrill you and make you believe, they don't bore you and make you wonder why you'd bothered. This may be hard for some Tottenham supporters to read but no one can begrudge what Arsene Wenger has done for Arsenal over the past two decades, despite the current situation. Indeed the unexpected win over Chelsea in the recent FA Cup Final was that combination of pragmatism and exciting football that most fans love.

At their best, the team played football that was a pleasure to watch, that has been to the benefit of the game and could make you sit back in wonder at what you'd just seen. OK, so he's a bit myopic where his players are concerned but so are many other managers. Spurs, under Harry, played similar football and White Hart Lane was a better place for it. Would you believe it, they're starting to do it again under Mr Pochettino? They just need to ease up on the passing back and let the football flow a little more.

The Barcelona team of a few years ago were even better than that with the path of the ball like a flow of water finding its way past those defenders who tried to prevent its passage. Much of the time there didn't even appear to be the abrupt change of direction that deflects the ball from one player to, another like lateral table tennis. Like I said, it flowed. Have you ever tried to stop the water in a stream by using your hands? The water ignores you and carries on regardless, finding the easiest way or weakest point to get through. That's how opposing defenders must have felt facing Barcelona. They were irrelevant to what the water would do whether they were there or not. Not surprising really when the coach's ethos was to play "in the future". By this is meant that the players are expected to know exactly where the ball is headed the moment it is passed. Interestingly, when Ron Greenwood was manager of West Ham in the late 1970's and early 1980's, that is exactly what he taught. Given my political viewpoint, it rather pleases me that this, the best football club in the world, is owned by its members. Who says that the free market is the best arbiter in everything?

Anyway, having rambled on about my footballing philosophy, I need to point out some of the obstacles to turning dreams into reality, one of which is the hire and fire mentality inherent in the game now. During the time that I have supported them, for example, including caretakers Spurs have had more managers than you could shake a stick at. The role call, including those caretakers, reads Bill Nicholson, Terry Neil, Keith Burkinshaw, Peter Shreeves, David Pleat, Trevor Harley and Doug Livermore, Terry Venables, Peter Shreeves (again), Doug Livermore (again), Ossie Ardiles, Steve Perryman, Gerry Francis, Chris Hughton, Christian Gross, George Graham, Glenn Hoddle, Jacques Santini, Martin Jol, Juande Ramos, Harry Redknapp, Andre Villas-Boas, Tim Sherwood and now Mauricio Pochettino. Apart from those in a caretaking role, only two left entirely of their own accord. The rest, I believe, were sacked.

Not taking the current manager into account and allowing for the fact that Billy Nick was manager for ten of those years, Keith Burkinshaw for eight, El Tel for five, Harry for four and Mauricio now, for three, the remaining managers were in charge for a total of twenty three years, or two less than the whole time that Sir Alex was at Manchester United. It works out at an average of roughly a season and a half each. Hardly the way to run anything successfully or even to run it at all. Yet, if the rumours that Fergie was approached by Spurs when he was manager of Aberdeen are true, could it have been different or would the board have sacked him within eighteen months? After all, it took three years for him to turn it round at Old Trafford, but what a turnaround it was. Was it worth the wait? Of course it was, in spades. Ask any United supporter, especially those watching the team today. I'm not saying that you don't sack people who aren't up to the job, rather, I'm questioning the judgement of those who appointed them in the first place.

One of the only saving graces is that there are other clubs that have been run worse than Spurs, allied to the fact that the club does, at last, seem to be starting to match team performance to sound finance. Itself, quite a juggling act. In a perverse fashion, what happens in football could be seen to demonstrate what many of us on the left believe. Business men (and they are invariably men) may be good at making money, some even at running a business. That doesn't mean to say that they are any good at anything else and certainly governments shouldn't treat them as though they automatically have a special expertise that extends beyond business into politics, running schools and other areas of life. They don't necessarily and we do them and society as a whole a disservice if we act as if they do. Political point over, back to the football.

Only a football club with a captive market could be run in this way; in any other sphere, the customers would have gone elsewhere. Yet we continue our support because our allegiance prevents us from doing anything else. So am I just looking at Spurs' history and thinking that those glory days still exist today or could again, if only? The answer is a categorical yes. Yes, Spurs were the only non league side to win the FA Cup in 1901. They were the first team in the last century to win the league and cup double. They were (almost) the first British team to win the old European Cup (and should have done), the first to win a European trophy (the Cup Winners' Cup in 1963) and so on. In reality, they haven't consistently been in the real elite in the modern era since, probably, the early 1970's and even before that only for about fifteen years. Indeed, just Bill Nicholson's reign. The rest, judged by the highest standards, has been "nearly" time. Inconsistently thrilling though much of it has been.

Yet the supporters, successive generations of them, fill the ground most weeks paying, these days, a not inconsiderable amount for the privilege. Yes, they sit now instead of standing but at a ground not well served by public transport. The same burgers, frankfurters, pies and chips are on sale, not cheaply, in the streets around the ground and the glory of the game is certainly not well represented by this environment. Could it be any different? Of course it could, why not? Keep Barcelona in mind. Good football that you own. However, let's not get too much beyond ourselves yet. All the more reason, though, why the football should be such that you believe the dreams are real, even if it's just for an hour and a half each week, summer not included.

Back down to earth, then, where it might be opportune at this juncture to consider Spur's playing record since the start of the season that I first watched them until I started this book a few years ago. During that time, other than friendlies, Spurs had played in the old First Division, had one season in the Second, been in the Premiership, the FA Cup and, what is now called, the Carabao Cup, the European Cup Winners' Cup, the Champions' League and the Europa League. According to Jim Duggan's excellent Topspurs website, there had been 2,313 matches of which Spurs have won 981, drawn 588 and lost 744. This breaks down respectively as 42.5% won, 25.5% drawn and 32% lost. Look at that last percentage; it means that they have lost one in every three games each season for the past 48 years and only won about 4 in very 10. Translating those figures to today's Premier League and Spurs will have picked up, on average, 57 out of a possible 111 points. That is not great by anyone's standards.

In the league, in only one of those seasons, 1977/8, have Spurs losses been down to single figures and, until this last season, their highest placing was 3rd in 1996/7 and 1984/5. Furthermore, in 28 of these 48 seasons, they have finished outside the top third of teams. That is not a record, for two generations, that should gladden the heart of any Spurs supporter. The school report says "Needs to do better". It should also, with the level of talent that has been available, say, "Should have done better". However, in an effort not to be too downbeat, an unfortunate trait among us older supporters, we can look at what was achieved and, in a later chapter, look at what has all the makings of being a considerably better future.

The record of this, previously, faded thoroughbred of a

club reads winners of the league (old First Division) in 1951 and 1961, FA Cup winners eight times in 1901, 1921, 1961, 1962, 1967, 1981, 1982 and 1991. Three European trophies starting with the Cup Winners' Cup in 1963, becoming the first English team to win a cup in Europe, and the EUFA Cup in 1972 and 1984. They have also won the League Cup, as it was first called, in 1971, 1973, 1999 and 2008. Now that is not a bad record by any standards. It is, however, still history and needs to be set against a background of a top four who, until a few seasons ago, were in danger of becoming a league in themselves.

Moreover, unless team like Spurs and Liverpool get themselves into real contention soon, there is a danger that the money the Champions League brings will mean that the gap gets ever harder to bridge. More and more money being circulated within a few European clubs could see a European League mirroring the Premiership. That is to say, an elite of four, mid table placings for 13 and relegation, usually from among those who have just been promoted, of three. Moreover, that situation could almost be cast in stone with the same teams in the same situation each season. At which point my usual cautious optimism reappears when I feel that Spurs now really have a better chance of remaining as one of that elite than they've had for as long as I can remember. That feels good. However, to do that the club has to keep this particular show on that road and maintain its momentum. If that happens, the "Audere est facere" will be more than just a Latin slogan.

If it does, it will demonstrate what I and many other many Spurs' fan believe; which is that quality matters. That answer lies in that tradition of trying to play the game as it should be played. I was brought up by, among others, an aunt who said that, if you do the right thing, you will get your rewards in life. However, if you measure those rewards in monetary terms and material success, it's simply not true, as must be obvious to anyone who has eyes to see. In the way she talked about it, though, it is very true. She meant, do what you think is right and you will get your rewards in the mere doing and, in that respect, she was correct. You have to live with yourself. Hence my support for Spurs. Back to

Danny Blanchflower again. For those who are interested, my Aunt Doreen also told me that a smile and thank you didn't cost anything and, moreover, could put a smile on the face of others. Not a bad philosophy for life that.

Yet had Roman Abramovitch turned to Spurs and not Chelsea all those years ago (and there are rumours), and appointed Jose Mourinho, would I have complained? I hope so; I did when it was George Graham. It wasn't his previous stewardship of Arsenal that was the problem. I just thought that the football was boring.

Is the Game Better Today?

The answer to that question is, in my view, a resounding 'yes' in just about every respect. It is faster and more tactical, players are fitter and more skilful and, as in the past, little quarter is given. Even the boots and ball are specially designed to provide greater accuracy and precision and, in doing so, push the levels of skills even higher. In the Premiership, players now come from all over the world to ply their trade and clubs scour the globe to uncover new, young talent ahead of their rivals. That is not to say that those special players in the past weren't that special or wouldn't have thrived in the modern game. Many would have done, George Best especially. It's just that the overall level of skill and ability has improved overall and, as a spectacle, the game is much the better for it.

This is reinforced by the improved facilities, although still not good enough in many grounds. Television coverage is fantastic; in high definition colour, you can see the most incredible close up action. Slow motion replays allow you to see things that were just too quick for the human eye, especially the biased one of a football supporter. Soon video replays will help referees to make the correct decision virtually every time. We'll even have televised football in 3D and not just on a flat screen but as if you were actually at the ground. Something that would have been within the realms of science fiction a few years ago, will be reality.

So, gone are the days, described so lovingly by Michael Parkinson, of heavy leather footballs, players ploughing through mud, steak and chips, cigarettes at half time and alcohol. These have largely been replaced by scientifically based training routines, diets and computer based studies and assessments of individual players' contributions or, in some cases, lack of contribution. We now know which players ran the furthest during a game, who provided most "assists" and all the other minutiae so beloved of statistic loving anoraks. Do these people not have a life and can they not just watch the game and enjoy the spectacle? Mind you, we've all watched games between two teams of pretty skilful footballers to which the word spectacle wouldn't apply by any stretch of the imagination. So, has it made for a better spectacle?

One way to answer that question, like much else in life, is would you want to turn the clock back and return to those times? I suspect the answer, for most of us, is no. Although we should beware rose tinted glasses, certainly life was simpler in many ways. People did, for example, know and speak to their neighbours much more. They did go out and leave their doors unlocked; even, in my former father in law's case, when he went on holiday for two weeks. What, until recently, has improved beyond measure, however, for most people in the UK, is material wealth and, in the case of sport, individual and team performances.

Athletes run faster and further, high jumpers, pole vaulters and long jumpers reach heights and distances previously undreamt of. People with disabilities and special needs are not only able to compete, instead of just being unacknowledged, but achieve beyond the abilities of most of the 80,000 spectators who cheered them to the echo at the Paralympics a few years ago. Women run marathons and in times not much less than their male counterparts thanks, for example, to such as Roberta Gibbs who, in 1966, was rejected by the organisers of the Boston Marathon. Women, you see were, considered, by international sports organisations, to be psychologically unable to run long distances; their competitive limit was 1½ miles. Roberta, clever person, sneaked in and completed the course in 3 hours 21 minutes and 40 seconds beating two thirds of the other, male, entrants in the process. And changing perceptions at the same time.

The questions that should be asked, however, are "Has there been a cost associated with that betterment and, if so, what is it?" Coupled with, "Has it been worth it?" For those who take life much as it comes, the answer to both these might well be "So what?" Life, after all, could be considered to be too short to worry about what might be and there is certainly some truth in that. Fortunately or unfortunately, I'm not one of those and I look at what might be. That way, maybe, the next generation can bring about greater change and not have to put up with what is left after those at the top table have taken what they consider to be their dues. So let's look at what might be the downside.

Well, professional football, in some ways, mirrors the society we live in. It is structured to ensure that the Premiership thrives while the grassroots, by default, do less well; a self defeating situation if ever there was one. Less expensive overseas players are brought in to the detriment of our own youngsters. Those youngsters don't progress as they might have done and the national team suffers as a result. The FA doesn't help by its unerring ability to choose the wrong manager for the national team. Interestingly, Patrick Vieira was recently quoted as saying that "For a big country like England, with the number of kids who love the game, you don't produce enough talent". He went on to say that he believed that one of the reasons is our coaching and that we need to review how to coach young people between the ages of 8 and 21.

Now you may feel that all this is inevitable much as was our country's decline from industrial powerhouse to somewhat lower down the international pecking order. I would argue that there is nothing inevitable and that something can always be done if there's a will. I would further argue that selling off the family silver, the clubs, is as silly a footballing policy as it is an industrial one. Yet, despite this, many clubs operate with an enormous level of debt. It is not the way run anything, let alone the country's national game. Do I expect it to change in the near future? Unfortunately, no.

So, yes, we have a more exciting and better game with increasing attendances; in England now rising to 29m from a low of 16m in the mid 1980's. Mind you, that does need to be set against the 41m figure for 1949! There are enormous rewards for the top clubs offset by enormous financial penalties for failure. Yet there are very significant downsides to all this success with real questions about its sustainability. In the meantime, we have the spectacle of wealthy owners taking over clubs with, it seems, little understanding of football management, the game itself or its significance in the lives of the communities in which the individual clubs are based. The fans, well, they're just the ones who turn up week in week out to watch the game. The depth of their identification with and feeling for their club being in marked contrast to that of its owners. It is a microcosm of the business world today and not a healthy one at that.

.

Matchday

Yes, you're probably thinking, but what about the game itself; when are you going to get around to that. Well, one of the reasons it's taken so long, other than that I wanted to write about all the other stuff first, is that, although I get just as emotional and excited about it as I always used to, I'm now somewhat more objective. There are reasons for that state of affairs, some to do with the game and some personal. I know that, when I was younger, I was much unhappier about my life and going to Spurs was a release. It probably meant that the contrast between the individual player's successes and my lack of any real achievement was even greater.

I put my unhappiness into that hour and a half each week or so during the season. It wasn't just a football match, it was an occasion and it partly made up for whatever was missing in the 166½ hours that made up the rest of my week. That didn't make it any less of an experience, probably quite the reverse. In addition, when I first started watching, there was very little live football on television. If you wanted to watch, you went to the game. Don't get me wrong, I love watching football from the comfort, usually, of the pub with a beer in my hand. Not only is it more convenient and comfortable, but you see so much more of the action in the most incredible close up. It is not, however, within the camaraderie of 40,000 or so other people all willing the same thing; that is, for the team to win with style. I must admit, though, I am now an armchair supporter except on the odd occasion that my son and I go together. Which is rarely these days.

So, what did it used to be like. Well football matches used to be played on a Saturday afternoon with the kick off at 3 o'clock or, for a midweek match, with a start at 7.30. Importantly, all the matches kicked off at the same time. You made your way to the ground along with every other fan in the country doing exactly same thing at the exactly same time. You had watched the lunchtime television footie programmes or listened to the radio to ensure that you hadn't missed anything and, it has to be said, to foster that emotional commitment that you had. It all helped to create an atmosphere, an expectation, of which the match was the culmination.

For home matches, you may have left home on your own. However, as you got nearer ground, others would join you, until, gradually, you stopped being an individual and became part of something greater. For me, walking from Weir Hall Avenue, that transition took place as I approached White Hart Lane Station. It was confirmed as I cut across the open land surrounding the block of flats in Love Lane where I hit the High Road before buying a programme. Being someone who hates missing out, I couldn't settle until I was through the turnstiles and in my usual place. First of all in the old enclosure and, later, in the corner of the Paxton Road end where I met mates. I could then settle down ready to enjoy the game or, at least, I hoped so.

Social life was built around the football, a life which, in those less enlightened times, was more based on the traditional roles that men and women were expected to fulfil. There was even a late edition of the evening newspapers specially printed to contain the football results and available by about six o'clock. The formal ending of the ritual which would, of course, then be discussed in the pub at lunchtime on Sunday and at work on Monday. For football fans, your week would be structured around the match with the tone for the following week set by the result.

It was a social ritual undertaken communally without any overall plan. Moreover, for me, it wasn't just about the time that you were in the ground, it was about that build up prior to the euphoria or disappointment that followed. For the big occasions, against Manchester United and Liverpool, I would aim to get into the ground at least half an hour and, on one occasion against United, an hour early, along with 58,000 others.

Floodlit matches had a special atmosphere about them. It was as if the surrounding darkness shut off the world outside, with the brilliance of the floodlights highlighting the pitch inside with even greater clarity than your senses. On cold evenings, the breath from the individual players made them seem even closer; their shouts to one another, louder. It really was a separate world from even those people who were less than a hundred yards away in the High Road. On those nights, the ground became a cocoon that you shared with the other supporters and the players on the pitch. The match officials, unless they made mistakes, never really figured much. You, the other supporters and your team were as one. They, with their endeavours, and you, willing them on. If you should think that the latter has little effect on the former, you should ask yourself why, over a season, teams always perform better at home than away. Which brings me to the game's aftermath.

The mind is a wonderful thing at the best of times. It is even more so in rationalising emotions, often, themselves irrational. In my experience, most of us are very good at rationalising the irrational and so it is with the supporters of football clubs. How could it be otherwise when the support itself is based on a form of tribalism, manifest in support for a particular club situated in a particular area made up of players from all over the globe? Many (and I mean many) years ago, the players may themselves may have been somewhat local. That is however, no longer the case. Even the fan base is broadening so that it is becoming worldwide. "Follow the money" always being the dictum. The ultimate irrationality is when players who previously turned out for a rival team and were, often, the subject of some animosity, are transferred and then turn up in the colours of your own club. Their misdemeanours, questions about their parentage, skills or sexuality are forgotten and you suddenly discover that, would you believe it, they are really very good. They become yours and you support them, largely.

So, in the immediacy of the moment, the result is the important issue although the emotions that are engendered will vary dependent on whether you are home or away and, to an extent, on the opposition. This variation will also likely be related to expectation. A home win, especially a handsome one, against the old enemy, will be greeted with euphoria. An away win, after being on the receiving end for much of the match, against the local rivals, will be greeted with ecstasy. Conversely, a home defeat against said local rivals or against greatly inferior opposition can bring frustration and, if you didn't play well, sheer bloody anger. Whereas, an honourable defeat at Old Trafford, another pedigree club, may elicit disappointment; an emotion that will be influenced by the fact that the team played well and "Well, it was United at their best". These occasions can even be reflected in admiration for the opposing team. Taking into account, of course, that your emotions will fluctuate wildly during the match and be affected by refereeing decisions, foul tackles and whatever else takes place during those 90 minutes. It can be an emotional rollercoaster of a ride.

Analysing the match with your mates at work on Monday lunchtime, especially if you had been playing the team that they support, or they had lost and you had won, was part of the ritual. I remember, after Spurs had played Liverpool and Gilzean had played a blinder, reading the description of his performance out to both a Chelsea and a Fulham supporter so that they could see that I wasn't as biased as they were indicating. I'm not sure that I was in complete control of my faculties at the time.

A good result could set you up for a few days, a bad one depress you. A fact now recognised by psychologists who have measured an increase in industrial production following good sports results. I know it's only a game but for many, it's more than that. It has something to do with identity and a sense of belonging and a common bond. It is probably what kept morale up at home during the Second World War. Certainly an aunt of mine seemed to regard those particular years as among the best of her life despite the fact that she was separated from her husband for most of the time and people were killing one another on an industrial scale. And before any of you make comments to yourself about marriage, they were very happy together.

One game that I didn't get into, probably fortunately, was the night Arsenal beat Spurs at White Hart Lane to win the double. I got no further that the road into the main entrance where, along with hundreds of others, I was trapped. At first, it wasn't too bad as we waited to see whether there was any chance of getting in.

However, as it got to nearer kick off time and it was obvious that there wasn't and with more people coming off the High Road, it got a little worrying. One young woman, I seem to remember, fainted and had to be passed overhead to the back of the crowd and safety. The rest of us had no such luck and had to put up with the crush, initially not so bad. Unfortunately, there seemed to be no one stopping people from coming off the High Road and our numbers swelled. Greater numbers in a space that didn't increase in size could only mean one thing and we were getting crushed. Gradually at first, I started to get really worried until the police decide to start pushing the crowds back into the main road and we all, I think, managed to get out safely. Only to learn, later, that Arsenal had, not only won at White Hart Lane but, in doing so, had set themselves up for the first double since Tottenham's historic win of 10 years previously. Not a good night all round.

52,000 saw the match with thousands more locked outside. Among the spectators was one Frank O'Farrell, then manager of Manchester United, who described the atmosphere as "the most electric for any match that I can remember". A 19 year old Ray Kennedy scored from a George Armstrong cross with three minutes left to play. Kennedy described it as the longest three minutes of his life. Five days later, Arsenal beat Liverpool in the FA Cup to win the double with a remarkable goal from Charlie George. No backlift with the ball powering into the net from 20 yards.

Misery indeed for any Tottenham supporter.

Those of you who follow the game will know what those feelings are. Those who don't are missing something unless, of course, they get it from some other activity in their lives. Yes, I can imagine what that might be but, at times, football can be a close run thing to sex and as a communal activity, better. Unless, of course, you like orgies.

What Makes a Good Team?

Although, nowadays, there is a lot more to it than just having a good manager, this is still a prerequisite. Without that person in place, one who knows what they are doing, commands respect and can get the best out of the players, you are unlikely to succeed. You can probably name teams who had good managers and didn't make it, I suspect that you would be hard pushed to find one without a good manager who did, good backroom staff notwithstanding.

I read somewhere, many years ago, that it took 25 back room staff to keep one frontline soldier in the field. That may have been an exaggeration but it does indicate that a high level of support is necessary to enable one person with the required expertise to do their job at the sharp end. Football may not be in the same league, but the players who turn out for the first team each week still represent the top of a pyramid; in the case of Spurs, in 2015/6, 409 staff for a first team squad of 33. That takes some managing and that's before you take into account injuries, form, morale and the personal and other problems that might affect a player's performance at any time. So, the starting point is that it's difficult to keep the show on the road running smoothly. Being successful at the highest level is something else.

Traditionally, in this country, the manager, among other things, pulled it all together on the field and ensured that the team performed to its collective best. There was a recognised first team with reserves of players who were, usually, not quite as good. There were certainly not the squads that we have today where, in some cases, clubs have nearly two full teams of top class players. The players themselves were also different in that they weren't well paid, lived reasonably locally and usually smoked and liked a drink or two. Those were, indeed, the days. Life was simpler then as, I suspect, was the job of football management.

Fast forward 50 years and you have multi disciplinary teams comprising coaches for individual positions, for fitness, for scrutiny of the opposition plus sports psychologists and whatever computer programme that coaches use to analyse just about everything that happens in a game. Don't get me wrong, the game is better for it but it does make the job of management more complicated. To this must be added players' ego's, their celebrity status and the intrusion of the popular press. The enormous financial rewards available to successful clubs and the intensity of the competition they generate only add to the mix. As does managing players from very different cultures who will, probably, not even speak the same language, at least, to begin with.

So, a new manager comes in, usually not in the most auspicious of circumstances, namely that the previous one has just been sacked and/or the team are either in danger of relegation or have not been performing as hoped for some time. Fortunately, it is likely that the whole management team will have been dispensed with, so the incumbent at least has somewhat of a free hand in selecting the rest of the coaching staff. However, considerable money will probably have been made available to the previous regime, which will likely mean that it isn't as readily available to the new one. As always in football, expectations are high and, lastly, in that small world, there will already be knowledge or rumours of the new manager's abilities. In these circumstances, making a good impression is pretty crucial. Whoever said that you don't get a second chance to make a first impression had it spot on. Winning immediately might not be an option. Showing that you know what you're doing certainly is.

Being liked, while not essential, can help; being respected, though, is essential as is being a leader. Together they are ideal. Forget it when people say that being disliked is unimportant. It isn't. Personally, I think that when people say that, it is just an excuse for bad behaviour and there's enough of that in the world as it is. You are, after all, likely to put in more effort for someone you like than dislike, while fear will only get you so far. The old adage that, if you have their balls, their hearts and minds will follow may have some truth in it; although quite what part of the body you are meant to tighten your grip on in the case of women's football is never specified. Motivation, in my experience, comes more from belief and encouragement. With just the occasional kick up the arse.

Yet, what a fan sees is a game in which there seems to be a dearth of managers of the necessary quality. In which the same old names, with the addition of the latest "must have" ones, circulate, are interviewed and appointed; a managerial merry go round. Those who make it and remain at the top level with the same club are very few and far between. In fact you could probably number them on the fingers of one hand. Not only that but the speed at which these people get on and off any particular club's merry go round is increasing. This hiring and firing almost at will, coupled with "trophy" ownership by oligarchs, isn't often the basis for success on the field. Yet it continues to be the professional game's modus operandum.

Some managers succeed in the short, medium and long term. Some succeed for a while only to find that, after four or five seasons, it all goes wrong. Some take a while to produce results and some don't at all. Some fail to make the leap from success at a smaller club to success at a larger one, an understandable situation. Some, however, don't succeed at a smaller club only to get the opportunity at a larger one where, unexpectedly, they do deliver. Robert de Matteo did this a few years ago making Chelsea Champions League winners for the first time. This, however, pales into insignificance compared to what Claudio Ranieri, deemed not good enough for Chelsea, did the season before last with Leicester. During the same season that his former club's manager, returning as "the happy one", was sacked after only one season, albeit one in which they finished up as League Champions again. At times, it can seem like a madhouse. So, is there a recipe for success and, if so, what are the ingredients?

For a start, the aforementioned manager, who will likely want their own choice of backroom staff. Anything from half a dozen upwards covering all those areas set out earlier and more. The management team will inherit players, many of whom have been brought in under the previous management, at some cost, and who may or may not be those the new manager would have chosen.

So the first problem is can you turn them from a group of individuals into a team, let alone a winning one and, if so, how? Can you get the players to play according to the tactics that you determine? Are you, as a manager, able to change tactics during the game if necessary, bearing in mind Terry Venables' reported quote that "It's at half time that a good manager earns his money". Do you have the players to change the game? Which ones need encouragement and which need a good kick up the arse? How do you deal with those who don't speak, in this case, English? Bearing in mind that the average Premiership player will have just over three weeks each season when they are injured, are any especially susceptible to injury? How do you accommodate a Dimitar Berbatov, one of my all time Spurs' greats and what happens if you don't? The combinations and permutations are almost endless. Having got the right players and the right tactics, playing in a team with a flexible approach that can defend and score goals, well, it's a start.

Directors of any company are those who are charged with running it. In business, they would, hopefully, have had experience of the particular business they are involved with plus other skills, eg finance, legal matters, sales, and personnel to name but a few. Football does, however, seem to attract more than its fair share of those whose involvement owes more to wealth, prestige and status than any love of the club or, even, knowledge of the game itself. This latter some-thing that has become even more obvious recently with the, sometimes, absentee, foreign ownership of many of our top clubs. It is not a healthy basis from which to manage a com-pany and, if Tom Bowers, in his book, "Broken Dreams", paints a true picture, can be a somewhat toxic mix. In addi-tion to these are the Chief Executive, Director of Football, if employed, and the office and other staff. So, a complex set of ingredients in themselves before how they are able work together is taken into account.

Finally there are the expectations; in some cases, dreams. Those of your employers (the board) being crucial. Those of the fans, less so, except where they get sufficiently over-whelming that they cause the board to take notice. A new manager with, usually, some of their own backroom staff steps into this mix and, in some cases, is required to do what no one else has previously done for the club. No wonder such people are few and far between. Of course most fans won't care too much about the manner in which their club is run. They will just want to see their team doing well. Unfortu-nately, like any business, the way in which it is run is likely to determine its results.

Now, in every walk of life, there can be quite a difference between the world of work on the shop floor and that of management. Indeed there are (and always have been) dif-ferent routes to each of these destinations. Unfortunately, good management requires a degree of practical experience, not just of management itself, but of the world within which that management is exercised. Professional football is to be commended in this respect as, at least at team manager and coaching level, those who are appointed are from the shop floor; that is that they've actually played the game at that level. No officer class or fast track university status for them when what is needed is practical experience. Are they, how-ever, themselves selected and employed by those with suf-ficient experience of the relevant issues? It would seem not as much as would be hoped.

Interestingly, another crucial factor, the ability to under-stand and get on with others, in order to take them with you, cannot really be taught. Reading Tom Bower's book about professional football gives the distinct impression that it is an area that could do with considerable improvement in some of the board rooms and the FA. Without it, the levers of power at the top may be operated but they will not be correctly connected up to the motivational engine that powers what happens below.

So, is professional football at the top level so different from any other area of expertise? In short, is the managerial merry go round at the top of the professional game inevitable? Well, little is actually inevitable except, of course, death, so the answer must be no. Until, that is, you take into account the circumstances under which that management operates. In this case, the short term, results driven, wealth oriented, celebrity, media intrusive culture that is professional football. It, almost inevitably, helps to create that merry go round.

Having written this, I'm aware that I've not actually written about what makes a good team but, rather, the difficulties involved in doing that and then sustaining it. In fact, I have written about the world in which clubs operate and the ingredients that are on hand to work with. Beyond that and the need for some reasonable degree of short term success, the aim should be to create an efficient, well run organisation with a good manager, a good back up team, good players and adequate finance. The manager needs to be supported by a board made up of people with direct experience of the world in which they operate and with sufficient knowledge to appoint the right person in the first place.

Finally, the system needs to be sustainable with the club setting up and operating one that perpetuates itself so that it can thrive under different managers for years into the future. The board then needs to let the manager and staff get on with it and provide the money to acquire the right players and a decent training academy to identify and bring the best young players to the club. It can be done, witness Liverpool and their "boot room" culture when, for many years, the club were extremely successful under a number of different managers with changes of personnel being relatively seamless. Are the demands of modern Premiership football and the culture within which it operates in this country, incompatible with that sort of system? Well, if they are, Spurs seem currently to be bucking the trend!

Tactics and Formations

It used to be so simple, 2-3-5, a goalie, two full backs, a
centre half and two half backs, with two wingers, one centre
forward and two inside forwards. One part of the team was
dedicated to stopping goals, one to creating them and one to
scoring them. I remember little in the way of tactics, at least
to the degree that they operate in the modern game. Except,
perhaps, at corners where the centre forward was expected to
help out the centre half; the one on his own side, that is.

The aim was to score more goals than the opposition with
each player's individual task clearly specified and described
so well by Michael Parkinson. Certainly the winger's job
was to beat the full back and get to the bye line to cross the
ball. The centre forward, in Parkie's immortal words, "was
expected to venture into enemy territory at least a couple of
times during the match and no one cared very much whether
he returned or not". The inside forwards were the thinkers,
the intellectuals of the game, usually slim and unassuming
in appearance. Assessing, plotting and executing. It was only
further back, starting at the half back line, that the rough

stuff took place. The area was peopled with hard men, two quite stocky and one tall, the latter to counteract the opposition centre forward in the air. The half backs were there to counteract the inside forwards and the full backs to watch the wingers. Full backs did not cross the half way line going forward and wingers did not cross it in the reverse direction.

These hard men were expected to make sure that their opponent didn't get past them, certainly with the ball and/or with all their limbs and faculties intact. Ideally, the opponent would find the ball taken from his feet in a manner that, if not quite kosher, then, at least, one where the referee didn't notice. If the half back was half good, they would take it forward, somewhat, and, if not, they would pass it to one of the team's intellectuals. These players' jobs were to create maximum damage by getting the ball to the wingers or the centre forward, the latter recognisable by his height and, according to Parkie, the fact that he wore that "haunted look". These half backs would take the ball and the player, fairly of course, while at the same time letting their opponent know that there was plenty more where that came from. The establishment of a pecking order, if you like. The full back's job was to take care of the opposing winger.

The last line of defence were the goalkeepers. The penalty area their province, solely under their command. Unless it was for corners, some seemed to regard any intrusion into the area, without permission, as a personal affront. They could be vociferous and, other than the captain, were the only ones on the pitch with the authority to give orders. In fact, in the penalty area, their superiority exceeded that of the team captain; this, one of the game's unwritten rules.

They were heroic, expected to be ever vigilant, inspire confidence and execute wonderfully dramatic saves when called upon to do so. They were never allowed to make mistakes and usually got the blame when the ball ended up in the net. Or, more likely, took the blame. This "blame under any circumstances" attitude also reflected in a certain mien. Utterly dedicated, probably obsessive, nonchalant or eccentric and, sometimes, a combination of all three. Within the team, they were probably the most individualistic, as indeed, they often were.

69

It should also be borne in mind that, in those days, substitutes weren't allowed and that, if someone was taken off injured, the team was down to ten men. Injured players, therefore, tended to stay on the pitch wherever possible, even if just for the nuisance value. With the goalie's unique set of skills, their replacement could be more problematic than that of an outfield player. Which, for those with very long memories, will bring to mind one Bert Trautmann. Bert was the Manchester City goalie who happened to be German and signed for the club in 1949, a few years after the end of the war. His claim to fame was that he played the last 15 minutes of the 1956 FA Cup Final with a broken neck. Perhaps it's a little unfair to make the comparison, as no one knew it at the time, but, perhaps, Jens Lehmann wasn't the first crazy German goalkeeper to play in English league football.

When I look at those old formations now, it is difficult to believe that teams lined up with, effectively, five forwards and, including the centre half, only three at the back. Tactics might, occasionally, have been based on Matt Busby's adage, "Just give it to George". No wonder there were scores of five all and, occasionally 10-4 and even 13-0. All of these, of course, at White Hart Lane.

So, when I first started to go to football matches, how the team would line up wasn't really discussed. That is not to say that teams didn't employ tactics, but that, when they did, it was within that standard formation of 2-3-5. Any discussion among the supporters would, more likely, be around how your full back would handle, say, George Best. It had worked well for so long. After all wasn't England regarded as the best team in the world, at least by the English, and hadn't Wolves beaten continental teams in the early 1950's with their typically English game? So, the defeat 3-6 of the national team, in November 1953, at Wembley, the home of football, by the Hungarians, came as a shock. Not so much because of the score, bad though that was, but by the tactics, a deep lying centre forward, that the Hungarians employed.

Something, however, must have already been stirring when Arthur Rowe's Spur's team won the old Second Division in 1949/50 going on to win the First Division two years later. They played something called "push and run" football. Interestingly, Rowe is said to have coached in Hungary before the war. Both, Bill Nicholson and Alf Ramsey, two footballers who were to play an important part as managers in the English game, featured in these Spurs teams. Five years later, in 1956, Manchester City won the FA Cup using the "Revie Plan" in which Don Revie played as a deep lying centre forward. Fast forward to 1961 and Spurs, under Billy Nick, playing push and run, became the first in the 20th century to win the league and cup double. Fast forward another five years and, playing 4-3-3, Alf Ramsey's "wingless wonders" won the world cup; something Alf had predicted, to widespread disbelief at the time. Modern tactics had arrived in England.

Despite this, the aim of the game still seemed to be to score more goals than the opposition irrespective of how many you gave away. It was, certainly, what I was used to. Until, that is, the Liverpool team of 1963/4 won the First Division Championship in only its second season in the top flight. I watched them and they seemed to think that preventing the opposition from scoring was more important than scoring themselves! This on the basis, if I understood it correctly, that a team that doesn't score can't win. Moreover, this was not just man to man but as a team, an organised unit. Had nobody read them the rules including the unwritten ones that Spurs adhered to?

To my great frustration at the time, it worked. Especially against Tottenham and often with a breakaway goal towards the end of the match; or so it seemed. They were a classic counter attacking team who would win, away from home, when the home side had had 80% of the play. It was bloody infuriating and what I saw as professionalism, a term later coined to describe how Don Revie's Leeds United played.

These teams, good at it though they were, were novices in comparison to the Italians who had been playing, and winning, using these tactics for years. All the more pleasure then to see Celtic beat the mighty Inter Milan in the 1967 European Cup Final in Lisbon after being 1-0 down. I watched it on television after rushing home from work early to see the Italians take the lead with a penalty and then try to frustrate Celtic. All out attacking football won that evening when Celtic became the first British team to win the European Cup with a team composed entirely of Scots. My faith in attacking football was, demonstrably, proven to be right.

Gradually, 2-3-5 and the attacking style of play that it produced was consigned to the dustbin of history. Spurs, with their possession football, should have been in their element. Unfortunately, they were too often, what Bill Shankly called, southern softies. Billy Nick's dictum that, if you had the ball, no matter where on the pitch you were at the time, you were attacking and, if the opposition had it, you were defending may have been true but defending itself gradually became the name of the game. Since then tactics and formations have changed a lot with 4-3-3, 4-2-4, 4-4-2, 5-4-1, 3-5-2, 4-1-4-1, 3-4-2-1. Plus how many more?

These have all developed in the middle ground of two tactical extremes, one being the Italian catenaccio system and, the other, the Dutch concept of total football. Catenaccio, the Italian word for bolt, was based on a method developed by an Austrian coach, Karl Rappan. Coaching the Swiss team in the years before and during the war, he used a player as a sweeper behind the rest of the defence. It relied on close man to man marking and was then taken up in Italy as early as 1947 with three banks of three players. Behind the last line of defence was a libero or sweeper taking care of anything or anyone who managed to get that far. Not many did, intact.

The famous Inter Milan coach Helenio Herrera developed this to its apogee in the 1960's so that a goal for his team usually meant that the match was over. That is what made Celtic's win all the more impressive. None of this should be taken to read that this wasn't "good" football although it could be frustrating to watch, especially for those of the opposing team. Mind you, a good sweeper was a cultured player who became the fulcrum of speedy counterattacks that followed. If you ever watched Bobby Moore or Franz Beckenbauer taking care of anything that did happen to get through and then initiating an attack, you saw an extremely cultured footballer.

The counterpoint was the total football credited to Rinus Michels, the Dutch coach in the 1970's. Played properly (and that takes skilled and dedicated players) it can make a team almost unplayable. Total football is what it says on the tin, a style where players can interchange in a fluid system over the whole pitch, making marking difficult. It is a joy to watch. I may be looking through extremely rose tinted specs here but there was a brief period under El Tel when I think Spurs played it. Looking back with, what, even for me, are the most rose tinted of spectacles, I remember, at least in my head, seeing Razor Ruddock on the right wing with the ball at his feet. Total football indeed, but did I really see it?

Nowadays coaches and managers employ an array of formations and tactics. Reinforced by ProSport, or whatever it's called these days, where a player's every move, with or without the ball, is recorded, it can sometimes feel as if the individuality is being squeezed out of the game. A reported comment from the Newcastle player to Big Sam, when he was manager of that club, would seem demonstrate that. After listening for some time to the manager describing how each individual opposition player played, one member of the team is reported to have asked "But how do you want us to play?" Like everything else in life, tools are meant to help but not to take over. I hope the result is not a game, like American football, with a series of set pieces and plays and cheerleaders on the pitch to enthuse the spectators. I thought that the game itself was meant to do that. Perhaps I am getting old.

Football Management

As a football manager, you operate in a world in which the media can veer from eulogy to castigation and back again, pretty quickly. "Turniphead" and the "Wally with the brolly" being just two examples of the latter. You also operate in a world where uninformed opinion becomes stated fact, as evidenced by the quote from one commentator on the radio, when Glenn Hoddle was manager of Spurs and with doubts about his abilities persisting, "What difference would a change of manager bring about and do what Hoddle couldn't do?" was asked. Obviously a comment either from someone who didn't want Hoddle sacked or someone who had never managed anything or both. A good manager can make all the difference in the world. Witness Manchester United under Alex Ferguson, Matt Busby, Bill Shankly, Bill Nicholson, Brian Clough, Jose Mourinho, even Harry, in the four seasons he had at Spurs and now, it seems, Mauricio Pochettino. What they did or are doing is no accident. If it was, why can't everyone do it? There's yet another PhD thesis in there.

Remember the famous First World War quote, "The

British fight like lions but they are lions led by donkeys". Well, a good manager can make lions out of donkeys and a bad one, donkeys out of skilled athletes. That's the difference. Gary Birtles was never the greatest player yet Brian Clough turned him into someone who Sir Alex was ready to pay good money for and then dispose of him when reality dawned. Yet I read somewhere that Sir Alan Sugar is supposed to have told Terry Venables that, if it didn't work you "Just get another geezer in". Venables is supposed to have responded that it wasn't that simple, "There weren't that many geezers." He was right, yet he too was eventually told, "You're fired!" Unfortunately, something of a catchphrase now.

The numbers of those who have been successful in the past and the fondness and respect with which they are remembered are testament to their abilities. Most football fans will remember every one and there will be a remarkable consensus as to who they were. We also, probably, remember the really bad ones, at least at the clubs we support. We tend not to remember the mediocre ones and those who, for whatever reason, never made it. Unless they themselves had been great players, when we wonder why it didn't happen for them. Bobby Moore, a wonderful footballer and the only captain of his country ever to lift the World Cup, springs to mind.

So, to reiterate, good teams are led by good managers and exceptional teams by exceptional managers. These latter being managers who can make average players into good ones and good players into excellent ones. Bad managers do the opposite. Good managers get the team working as a unit, bad ones as a series of individuals. In Tottenham's case in previous years, occasionally like headless chickens. You probably remember the matches better than I do. Which brings me to another point; a team needs a manager on the pitch as well as in the dressing room, something else that Tottenham have often lacked over the years. Maybe it would have been different had Ledley played more often. He wasn't just a great defender, he inspired, just by his presence. At Tottenham, all those years ago, it was Danny Blanchflower, then Dave Mackay and, later, Alan Mullery and Gary

Mabbutt, all leaders on the pitch, albeit with differing styles.

So, what makes a manager? Well according to Arsene Wenger, although football management has changed dramatically in the 30 odd years since he took up his first post, the fundamentals of being a successful manager remain the same. These are a passion for the sport, the management of people, the ability to evolve and adapt and an eye for talent. You could also add what he has done and what Mauricio Pochettino has done at Spurs, which is the ability to create the culture that a successful club requires. Both these men, incidentally, believe that winning needs to be the consequence of excellence rather than its sole justification. In that they differ from some other managers, none of whom feature in my list of the managerial "greats". Finally, although no great manager leaves things to chance, luck also plays a hand.

So, how do you go about finding a good manager? Now, as someone who has never met a football manager, I realise that I am making myself a hostage to fortune by continuing along this route. However, I have some experience of successful management and recruiting people and, as I am a follower of the game writing about how I see it, here goes. Interestingly, a few years ago, I happened to meet a former international footballer running a pub in Yorkshire. He was no longer in the game and I wondered why. How, for example, did you get to be a manager? "Simple" he said without any noticeable animosity, "football's old boy network", quoting one particular former international who was considerably less successful as a manager than as a player. I think the word "whingeing" was used. If that is so, and it has the ring of truth about it, it explains a great deal.

This network is also confirmed by someone who writes under the pseudonym of "The Secret Footballer". In his first book he writes that unless you know someone in the game, it will be extremely difficult for anyone to get into coaching at any level. Coupled with the comment from Mr Venables about they're not being many geezers and you have a problem. So, is there an answer and, if so, what is it?

Well, you start by realising that no board of Directors deliberately sets out to choose someone who is not up to the job. Yet, too frequently, they seem to do just that. I wouldn't want to lay myself open to libel but we all know the names that appear whenever a vacancy arises and you think "What?" Now I am very conscious that this may be just newspaper talk. However, too often managers fail at one club only to reappear at another with remarkably similar results. Having interviewed a fair number of people to fill job vacancies, I know that there can be a group dynamic created among those interviewing and that a system needs to be in place that helps them to make objective decisions.

One can only come to the conclusion that something is not as good as it needs to be in the world of selecting football managers. As I've previously written, Spurs don't have a good track record in this area. At the start of the current season and since it was created 25 years ago, of those currently now in the Premiership, Spurs, with 20, are second only to Southampton with 21. Only eight clubs are in single figures in this field, among them Arsenal, with four and United, with seven, although the latter have since had three in three years. Either the job at that level is nigh on impossible or those who appoint managers in the first place aren't that well equipped to do so. Possibly a combination of both.

So, what is needed? Well, a proven track record at the same level of football or the demonstration that they can make the step up from where they are now. That record should not only be of success in circumstances similar to those that your own club operates in, but with a style that you would want that success to be achieved by. The chances are that someone who has already achieved will achieve again. Remember, however, to take into account the circumstances under which they achieved. Malcolm Allison and Joe Mercer were a great double act for Manchester City in the late 1960's, Malcolm Allison less so on his own. Even the great Brian Clough was not as good without Peter Taylor, at least when they first split up. Mind you, what he did afterwards put all his previous achievements in the shade.

A manager also needs, quickly, to demonstrate some ability while taking the players and the board with them, a difficult juggling act. Either that or, like Sir Alex, they and the board need to hold their nerve in getting rid of certain players, no matter how powerful and influential they might be. So, how do you get a track record if you don't already have one? Well you have to start somewhere. Cloughie started with Hartlepool, for heaven's sake, with all due respect to the club. Whatever he did there (and I understand that, because there was no money, he even turned his hand to painting the stands) it must have demonstrated something. If you are good organiser who gets on with things, prime requirements for management, it will usually show at whatever level.

Also, at the top level of the game, the job of management has changed considerably over the last 30 years. One man bands, some of whom are among the all time greats that my generation grew up with and who I describe later in this book, always were few and far between. In the more corporate world that is professional football, and much else today, just the sort of difference that their, somewhat, individual style brought, is less likely to be tolerated, no matter how successful they are. Jose Mourinho and Harry Redknapp being just two high profile examples. Ironic really that just what is needed is less likely to be tolerated at least in the longer term. Perhaps this helps to explain the much reduced managerial tenure that operates within professional football which, in the Premiership, now stands at 2.7 years. This translates as a little over two seasons. When you consider the fact that three managers, Sir Alex, Arsene Wenger and David Moyes had 52 years between them, the average for the rest is somewhat less. Mind you, the latter has had considerably less success since leaving Everton.

Above all, have a plan B and don't let your desperate need to get someone, anyone, override your judgement. As Marlon Brando once said, "Just because they yell "Action", it doesn't mean that you have to do anything". If you have just sacked your manager (and have a history of doing that), it doesn't necessarily mean that you have to appoint another one without giving some consideration as to why the last one (and the one before that and the one before that, etc, etc.) failed. Does this sound familiar, Spurs supporters? It's not as if the grapevine in football doesn't exist. It's a small world and I find it difficult to believe that word doesn't get around about what managers and potential managers are like. Indeed, as the former international footballer explained, they do. Yet, for some reason, viewed from the outside, football does seem to operate in a bubble and that may be part of the problem.

It's an interesting point, but worth mentioning, that many top managers were not themselves players at the highest level or, as in the case of Brian Clough, had a promising career terminated by injury. Do they feel that they have something to prove? Furthermore many of the best players did not succeed as managers to the degree that their playing careers might have led them, and others, to expect. Bryan Robson, Roy Keane, Glenn Hoddle and Tony Adams to name but a few. Why should this be so? One answer might be that those with the greatest skills and determination find it difficult to understand that others don't necessarily have these. Kevin Keegan, not the most naturally gifted of footballers, got where he did by no little skill reinforced by dedication, hard work and sheer bloody effort. I always thought that, as a manager, he couldn't understand players who weren't willing to do the same. It's what he did and what got him to where it did, so why couldn't others do it? Well some do or will and some can't or won't.

It may be an obvious statement but when a new manager takes over a team, he inherits what he has which is not usually the same as what he wants. He will inherit a dressing room that may or may not be harmonious. Motivating these individual players, some of whom he may not hold in high regard, especially when they may be earning more than him, cannot be easy. When some of them seem to have their brains in their boots and may not even speak the same language, it must be even more difficult. It probably explains why many of these managers go for those players that they know and trust as much as their inherent skill. Perhaps, though, it explains Terry Venables' comment about there "not being many geezers".

Great managers have vision and the ability to make that vision real in a world where great skill and artistry meet defensive skulduggery. In theory, it's not rocket science. However, it is difficult to put into practice and even more difficult to do that successfully and that's before you consider boardroom politics. The best managers, however, should always have that dictum of Danny Blanchflower's in mind. Which takes me back full circle to "Why Spurs?" Do I deliberately support, what has been a good but "nearly" club for much of that time, and, if so, why?

The answer to that lies, as I have said previously, in what I believe Spurs to be, which is a club that likes to play with a certain style. Blanchflower again. West Ham are the same, as are United. Spurs and West Ham less successfully but United certainly so and not just with Fergie. Although, as expected, they have had great difficulty replacing him. Would I swap Spurs' style for winning at all costs? Well, when they do win, almost yes but, no, not really. The means is as important as the result, the journey as important as the destination. Try a canal holiday or go cycling and you will see why. In a car, the destination is important, the route less so other than it being the most direct, easiest or cheapest option. With the other means of travel, what you will remember is the journey itself, the scenery on the way, for its own sake. Similarly with football. Mind you, so is the result if I'm brutally honest.

The Players

Now for the gladiators, those few people who get the chance in life to strut their stuff in front of thousands. Well, as with managers, there are bad players, mediocre players, average players, good players, very good players, excellent players and outstanding players. Just occasionally, there are geniuses. The latter being those who make the hair stand up on the back of your neck with their outrageous talent, who do things that you can't believe even when you've just seen it with your own eyes. These players mesmerise. They do the impossible and they make the difficult look simple. Some even appear to slow down time with their skill. Put the ball somewhere in the general direction of their feet in the middle of a crowded penalty area when you can't even see where it is for the bodies and the flying boots and they will come out the other side, with the ball at their feet and put it into the back of the net.

Some are players who can see the whole picture in their head at any time during the game and know just where, when and how to make that pass, sometimes half the length of the pitch and more, that cuts out most of the opposing defence in an instant. Moreover, they have the skill and ability to actually play that pass, not necessarily the same thing. Some have that focus that only sees ball and goal and the imperative that puts the former into the latter, time and again.

Great players can dictate and, literally, change a game and are the true artists. Michelangelo in football boots. Fortunately for Michelangelo, he didn't have Ron Harris, Norman Hunter or today's equivalent kicking lumps out of him while he was painting the ceiling of the Sistine Chapel. Just as well really that it was the ceiling and not the skirting boards. I suspect, however, that there was a bureaucratic thug below trying to ruin it. After all, it's always easier to destroy than create which is why defenders usually have the whip hand.

Others are great because, although they might not have the breathtaking skill, they do have the courage, determination and sheer bloodymindedness to take a game by the scruff of the neck and drive it forward in the way they want. When things are not going as planned and the opposition are imposing their will, players like this will step up to the plate and make their presence known. They can run through brick walls. Indeed, they probably aren't even aware that the walls are there. Flying boots don't put them off nor do vicious tackles, elbows or whatever is utilised in an effort to stop them. It doesn't. These are the legends of the football field, each one a colossus. Any football supporter will have their own list and the chances are that the player at the head of one person's list will head the "villains" list of their nearest rivals. Which saves me mentioning football villains except for Robbie Savage who is on everyone's list under "villain, pantomime". It's a role that he's worked hard at and, I think, rather enjoys.

Although some footballers have skills that take your breath away (see the next chapter), those who do make it to the top get these through a combination of skill, hard work and practice. Witness David Beckham and Kevin Keegan. How many hours did Beckham practice to be able to put that ball into the precise spot in the net or onto someone's head or feet where he wanted it to go? I doubt whether Kevin Keegan would consider himself the most naturally gifted of footballers, yet through sheer dedication and hard work, he made himself into the footballer he became, winning European Footballer of the Year in the process. Among the current crop of Premiership players Harry Kane springs to mind as the epitome of the virtues of skill and hard work.

I am also reminded of, I think, Jack Nicklaus who was told by an interviewer that he was a lucky golfer. He is said to have responded that "It's funny but the harder I train, the luckier I get". Similarly with Kevin Keegan, a player so fit he would run and run until his opponent gave up exhausted. It's also probably true that he couldn't understand why some of the next generation couldn't do the same. It's a fault that many dedicated people suffer from as they get older.

Although it is usually the goal scorers and skilful play-makers that catch the eye, defenders too should not be underestimated. Bobby Moore evidently was not very fast nor very good at heading a ball. That didn't stop him from, at one time, being the best defender in the world. Beckenbauer was a defender of class as was Paulo Maldini. All three had an aura of calm and quiet invincibility, probably because they were just that, calm and invincible. Lots of people talk the talk, these walked the walk at the highest levels throughout their careers and will be remembered for it long after they have stopped playing or are even still alive.

Goalkeepers are different although it probably helps to be slightly mad. After all who else throws themselves in the way of a foot, with a boot fitted to it, drawn back ready to be unleashed with some power, somewhere in the direction of their head? Who reaches above their head in a crowded penalty area to grab a ball when the mere act of that extension of both arms, leaves their body totally unprotected when others around them are determined on one thing? They want that ball as much as you do and are not above a bit of gamesmanship and physical violence to get it. Who ultimately get the blame when the ball goes into the net that they are guarding? It's called a hiding to nothing and yet people do it, many of them exceptionally well and, seemingly, not mad.

So well, in fact, that they take your breath away. Gordon Banks saving from Pele's header probably being the ultimate. Directed with power from above the defender, down towards the bottom corner of the goal from point blank range. Somehow Banks got to it to push it around the bottom of the post. Unbelievable. Even now, nearly 50 years later when you watch it, you still think the ball is going over the line. It isn't and it didn't. That save defied the laws of science. Your eyes got it wrong, except that they didn't. Banksie saved it. Mind you, Brazil did go on to win the match.

Many years ago Michael Parkinson wrote an article describing how the individual players in a team were expected to play. Typical of Parkie's writing on football, it was classic. I can't remember everything he wrote but the parts that I do remember are worth quoting, I hope accurately. He wrote of "teams having two wingers, one bandy legged, tricky and Scottish and the other fast, direct and Welsh. The centre half had a forehead hammered flat from contact with a thousand muddy balls and memorably, the centre forward, who bore the haunted look of a kamikaze pilot. He knew that he would be expected to venture into enemy territory at least twice during the match and no one knew or even cared very much if he ever came back". Skinner Normanton, who played for Parkie's beloved Barnsley was bald and, trying to head the ball away, had it skid off his pate. A voice from the crowd could be heard, "Put some chalk on t' cue, Skinner". Great writing, portraying a picture of a world that everyone then understood. Real and surreal at the same time.

For my generation, that article encapsulated football as it was then, an era when the game was rooted in its community. Played, often, not on grass but, for much of the time, on mud, with a leather ball and with the players wearing long shorts and heavy boots. It was an era of fags and Brylcreem, relatives living and working in close proximity, men being men and women doing the housework and no extra marital sex, officially that is. I know I exaggerate somewhat but that is how it felt. Family rituals and rites of passage existed, demonstrated, in my case, when the "News of the World" stopped being delivered when I reached the age of 11 because I might then understand what it contained and, more importantly, ask questions. So the picture of a more ordered, more conventional society was certainly an accurate one.

That community is now gone for most of us in the west. We now live in a global village; football included. And, yes, the game is greatly superior in individual technique, team-work, tactics, and speed and beamed directly into our homes in close up detail. I believe that the game is better for these things although part of me also feels that something has been lost in the process. True, or the thoughts of a previous generation? A bit of both really.

The Best Spurs' Players of My Time

Indulge me, if you will, but I cannot but include something on my choice of Spurs' best players during the 53 years that I've supported the club. Unfortunately, even someone of my, somewhat, advanced age, never saw Danny Blanchflower or John White play; two players who might have been included in anyone's list of all time greats. Perhaps if I hadn't been in the army in Germany, I might have done, but that, as they say, is life. Fortunately for me, I did see the greatest player ever to come out of these islands. The late, great George Best. Artistry in human form not, in my humble opinion, seen since. Although not a Spurs player he did grace White Hart Lane frequently during my time, so more of him later.

So, how the hell do you decide, when there have been so many? Well, I've relied on that old standby, personal choice; those I liked. So, on that basis, here is my list of candidates in, I think, historical order and, remember, it's my list and not yours and more people will disagree with it than agree. Also, please bear in mind the tendency of older people to be nostalgic. So here goes and, coincidentally, it's a team's worth of players plus reserves:

Cliff Jones, Dave Mackay, Jimmy Greaves, Alan Gilzean, Pat Jennings, Ossie Ardiles, Richard Gough, Glenn Hoddle, Paul Gascoigne, Teddy Sheringham, Jurgen Klinsmann, David Ginola, Dimitar Berbatov, Luka Modric, Gareth Bale.

And, just in case, you think I'm reminiscing too much, the current team comprises a number of players who will be on any list that I might make in 10 years time; notably Delli Ali and Harry Kane, to name but two.

With the possible exception of Berbatov, all these players won the hearts of the supporters as well as thrilling them. Even he did until his transfer to Manchester United under circumstances that left a slight taste in the mouth. In any intellectual or artistic endeavour, some would have been described as geniuses. Gascoigne certainly was. Troubled, maybe, but a talent so outrageous that, it seems other top class players, at a training session, watched, silent and in awe, spontaneously applauding what they had just seen him do. Some accolade that.

Cliff Jones

I used to pass a shop on the way to the ground with a sign over it that read, if I remember correctly, Cliff Jones, Butcher. It was in that little parade of shops on White Hart Lane just before the station. Well the sign may have read "Butcher" but it should have read "Wizard" and a brave one at that. Fast, direct, accurate, able to beat an opponent with ease and a good header of the ball who was not afraid to put that head where others put their boots, as I saw him do.

A member of the double winning team, he was regarded by many as the best left winger in the world at that time. Born in Swansea, he played for the town and was brought to Spurs by Bill Nicholson in 1958. Capped for Wales 59 times, he scored 16 goals for his country, regarding one of these, it is said, as the best he ever scored. My abiding memory of him is of an evening match under floodlights when he went past the full back as if he wasn't there, took the ball to the bye line and centred with precision. He was so close I could have reached out and touched him as he went past and I remember that he was smiling as he ran. I think it was the same match where he went for a flying header at the near post for a ball that the opposing defenders were trying to clear with their feet. The potential danger didn't seem to have occurred to him. Putting the ball in the net did.

After ten years, Cliff left White Hart Lane for Fulham moving on again, after two seasons, to Kings Lynn and Wealdstone before becoming a PE Teacher at Highbury Grove School. If only they knew it, those children were blessed by the presence of someone special. He is still involved with Spurs over fifty years after his final game for the club and I saw him on the pitch at a match against West Brom a few years ago. He didn't seem to have changed much, although he was fifty yards or more away at the time, so maybe that and my rose tinted specs helped.

Dave Mackay

If you wanted one person on your side in a battle, it would be Dave Mackay. Described by Brian Clough as Tottenham's greatest ever player, he probably was. The defining image of Dave Mackay (and one that he hated) is that one of him holding Bremner by the front of his shirt at White Hart Lane after the latter had overstepped the mark and, yes, I was there.

Jimmy Greaves is reported to have said that "He went into battle like a warrior" and that "he was the best professional that I ever worked with". Cliff Jones says that "Once Dave Mackay settled into that number six shirt, he turned a good side into a great one". Younger readers, if there are any, may see a resemblance to Roy Keane. I think Mackay was better.

Hard man he may have been but he sure knew how to play football. Regarded by the manager as his greatest ever signing, he was the heartbeat of a team that many romantics regard as the best of the 20th century. Whether defending or driving forward, he was the engine of the team and the midfield partnership of him and Danny Blanchflower would take some beating at any time.

After joining Spurs in 1958, he was a member of the double winning team, eventually becoming captain and guiding the club to the FA Cup, again, the following year. Then, on a winter's evening at old Trafford in December 1963, he broke his left leg. When it happened, Greavesie said that "the heart of the double side went with him. We were never the same again. Somehow the magic had gone". Yet, even as he was carried off, he propped himself up on his left elbow. He must have been in agony from a double fracture but was damned if he was going to admit it. That was Mackay's way. Show no weakness and tell yourself that you will win. With that attitude, you probably will and, moreover, others will believe you and that's half the battle.

It was feared that, at 29, his career was over. His determination ensured that it wasn't until a second fracture of the same leg the following season. Even that, however, didn't stop him. Neither did Billy Bremner on August 20 1966, weeks after England had won the World Cup. It was the opening match of the season against Leeds United when, infuriated by a kick from the said Bremner, on the same left leg, calculated, many thought, to damage it again and put Mackay out of the match, he retaliated. Captured in that famous picture. What is notable in this is Bremner's "hands held out" gesture indicating a desire to ensure that no further damage resulted only, this time, on himself. It is the gesture of one who knows that he has overstepped the mark and who had better make sure that the harder player knew that. One, believing himself to be an alpha male, being put in his place by one real alpha male. Despite the fact that we profess not to like retaliation, for a Spurs supporter, it was bliss. As was the result on that sunny afternoon, Spurs beat Leeds 3-1 in front of 43,844 people, with goals from Alan Mullery and the G Men, Greaves and Gilzean.

I travelled to Wolves to watch his last league match for the club. A crowd of us went in a minibus, with driver, supplied by one of the lads' fathers who owned a car hire firm. I don't remember much about the match or even the result although the journey back had its moments. After drinking till nearly closing time, we got into the van to be driven home. I fell asleep almost immediately to wake up about an hour and a half later. Dave Ellingham asked me, with a smile on his face, if I knew where we were. I looked at my watch and thought that it might be somewhere near London. "No", he said, "We're still in Birmingham. The driver has been driving since picked us up. He has been driving around the same roads again and again and he's lost".

Even in those days, I knew that you didn't get anything done by doing nothing and told the driver to pull over so we could try to work on how to get to the motorway. Fortunately, a police car came by and, after we'd explained our situation, one of the occupants said, "Follow us, lads, we'll get you there". Which they kindly did. At last, we all thought, we're on our way. It was not to be. The driver had driven round so long that we ran out of fuel and had to get to a garage somewhere to collect a can full. We got home, I think, sometime about two am with my wife frantic and me, probably, promising never to travel to an away match again. Along with the imminent departure of the club's icon, it was not an auspicious occasion.

After captaining the team to an FA Cup Final win against Chelsea in 1967 (I was at that one too), Dave Mackay was made available for transfer in 1968 and was snapped up by Brian Clough who supposedly waited in the corridor at White Hart Lane for some hours to make sure that he got his man. The rest, as they say, is history. In his first season with the club, as a sweeper, he helped Derby to gain promotion to the old First Division and later went on to greater heights. Stints with Swindon, as player manager, and Nottingham Forest followed until, in October 1973, following

Brian Clough's resignation, he returned to the Baseball Ground.

Under his management, Derby won the 1975 league title and put in creditable performances in the league and FA Cup in the following seasons before the great man was sacked in November 1976. He moved around to other clubs in the succeeding years before retiring from football in 1997. He died in March 2015, aged 81 having had, a few years previously, surgery and radiotherapy. When asked about his health at that time, he replied "Och a wee touch of cancer or something, no problem" in that quiet voice of his that belied the warrior within. They really don't make them like that anymore.

Interestingly, for those who like their Ronnie Barker, a newspaper with the headline "Mackay sacked" was used in the television series "Porridge". This series featured an actor named Fulton Mackay, another Scot, as Mr Mackay, a prison warder.

James Peter Greaves

Jimmy was simply the best goal scorer I ever saw. If you wanted the ball to be put into the net, consistently and with no mean skill, against any opposition, then you could virtually bank on him to do it. Signed by Chelsea at the age of 17 in 1957, he moved to AC Milan in 1961. Unhappy there, he was snapped up by Spurs in the same year, supposedly for £99,999 as Bill Nicholson didn't want him labelled the first £100,000 player. Seems peanuts today when journeymen go for millions.

He scored on his debut for all the clubs he ever played for and, by 1960, became the youngest player, at just short of 20 years of age, to score 100 goals in English league football. He went on to become the top scorer in two of his three seasons at Chelsea and his record of 41 goals in his last season is still a club record. Following his move from AC Milan,

Jimmy enjoyed a career at Spurs, from 1961 until 1970, that is legendary. In 379 matches, he scored a club record of 266 goals. He finished up as the top scorer in the league in the seasons from 1963 until 1965 and again in 1969 while his record at Spurs has only been matched once, by Clive Allen.

I was lucky enough to have the years that I got watch Spurs regularly coincide with his great years. Operating largely in the penalty area where football's hard men live with the madman of the team guarding the net, he thrived. Like a wild animal feeding in the vicinity of predators, he kept his senses on full alert, moving, ever vigilant, ready to make the crucial strike that would achieve his one aim. Putting the ball in the net. He, you see, was the real predator. Having scored, he would then wheel away from the goal, his job done. Until the next time when he would again scamper into the penalty area to repeat the process. Consistently, week after week, throughout his career. A goalscorer par excellence and a joy to watch, especially for any Tottenham supporter during the 60's.

Jimmy left Spurs for West Ham in 1970, where, as ever, he scored on his debut. Two goals against Manchester City, as you ask, towards the end of the season. He retired the following year having scored 516 matches in the Football League scoring 357 goals. At the age of 38, he made a comeback for Barnet where he played in midfield. Despite this, he scored 25 goals and was voted the club's Player of the Season. He went on to play for Woodford Town before finally giving up the game he had graced for so many years. Years later, I met someone who said that he had played against a team that had included Greavsie after he had retired. He told me that he looked at this overweight figure, out of condition and thought, "We'll stop him". He laughed when he said that Jimmy couldn't run much but knew exactly where the goal was and how to put the ball into the back of the net, which he did. Some things you never forget.

He is arguably, the most consistent goal scorer in the history of English football and stills holds the record of finishing as top scorer in the league in six seasons. Christiano Ronaldo he was not. Instead he was someone who got on with a job he thoroughly enjoyed without any flashiness or great histrionics. I heard somewhere a, probably, apocryphal story which I like to think is true. Someone was discussing the fact that, despite having lumps kicked out of him, he never retaliated. His response was that he did indeed retaliate, he put the ball in the back of the net. True or not, it sums up one James P Greaves, Tottenham and English football's greatest ever goalscorer.

Unfortunately, Jimmy suffered a stroke a while ago and is now confined to a wheelchair; at which point the mortality of a youthful hero brings your own into sharp focus. Thanks for the memories, Jimmy.

Alan Gilzean

This one is for old time's sake. Gilly is included because he was the first player I noticed who did things differently. A Dimitar Berbatov before his time. Supposedly known in his native Dundee as a dicer, ie one good game in six, he was anything but. That being said, he did have his off days but he played football with feints, flicks, back headers and a whole array of skills that I hadn't seen before. Bear in mind, I was new to football at that time. He even, on one occasion, if I remember correctly, nutmegged Bobby Moore down by the left hand corner flag and, on another from a corner, backheaded over the defender to score, against a Liverpool team then in their prime. I had never seen such a header before. His partnership with Greaves, as one half of the G men, provided Spurs with more than their fair share of goals in the seasons 1964 to 1970.

After playing for a series of local sides, Gilly joined Dundee in January 1956 as an amateur before signing professionally at the start of the 1957/58 season. He went on to score over 100 goals for the club helping it to win the league championship in 1961/2. He made his first international appearance in 1963 and is said to have first come to Tottenham's notice when, playing for a Scotland Select XI in a memorial match for John White, he scored twice. He signed for Spurs in December 1964 making his debut against Everton at White Hart Lane. The first match I ever attended.

When Greaves left, six years later, Gilly was partnered with Martin Chivers, an enigma in a white shirt, if ever there was one. After helping the club to win the League Cup (twice) and UEFA Cup, Gilly retired at the end of the 1973/4 season and, with his departure, went a truly skilful player who showed this supporter a more thoughtful approach to the game. Gentle glancing headers, flicks of the ball, feints and a reading of the game that was superb. Gilly is still fondly remembered by Spurs supporters of a certain generation. For others, find, if you can, the archives from The Observer of a match against Liverpool at White Hart Lane, on a warm Saturday afternoon, in the middle of the 1960's for a wonderful description of the skills and abilities of Alan Gilzean, footballer par excellence.

Pat Jennings

What can you say about the man who replaced the great Bill Brown in goal other than that he was the best Spurs goalie of my time. Making it all the more inexplicable that Spurs should transfer him to their arch rivals in his prime. Pat made very few mistakes and, with his positional sense and agility, was the custodian of the Spurs penalty area from 1964 for 13 years. Heaven know how many shots on goal he saved with those extraordinarily large hands. Sometimes, where others would tip the ball over the bar with their fingertips, he would save with one hand. At least that's how I remember it. One save, against Newcastle, if my memory serves me well, on the volley, at point blank range and at full power was blocked with his body. Outstanding. To complete the picture, in the 1967 Charity Shield match, he even managed to score one from his own penalty area much to the embarrassment of Alex Stepney, Manchester United's goalie at the time. The match ended in a 3 -3 draw. In 1973, he was named Footballer of the Year by the Football Writers' Association and, in 1976, won the Professional Footballers' Association version of the award.

Thinking that, at 32, he was nearing the end of his career, Spurs transferred him to Arsenal in August 1977. Unfortunately for the club, he wore the Arsenal jersey for a further eight years helping them to win three successive FA Cup finals between 1978 and 1980. Terry Neill, then Arsenal manager, described the deal as "One of the best transfer deals I made during my career" whereas Keith Burkinshaw, his Spurs counterpart, admitted that it was one of the worst decisions he ever made.

So having made 591 appearances for Spurs, he went on to make a further 327 for his rivals. The latter not bad for a goalie nearing the end of his career. To this can be added the 119 matches he played for Northern Ireland. A total of over 1,000 matches at the top level before you take into account Watford and Newry Town. He retired from first team football in 1985 and returned to Spurs, playing in the reserves so that he could be fit for the 1986 World Cup campaign. Pat went on to become a goalkeeping coach at Spurs and, in recognition of his achievements, was inducted into the English Football Hall of Fame in 2003. Having achieved his ambition of playing in the World Cup in 1982, Northern Ireland again qualified in 1986 when Pat made his final appearance for his country against Brazil on his 41st birthday. Nine years after someone at Tottenham decided that he was at the end of his career!

Ossie Ardiles

Ossie came to Spurs just after winning the World Cup for Argentina in 1978. He and Ricky Villa were signed jointly by Keith Burkinshaw, a masterstroke, under the noses of everyone else. Tommy Smith is supposed to have said that Ossie wouldn't last a winter in England and he may even have been a makeweight in the deal for Ricky Villa, a player with "legs like tree trunks" who could plough skilfully through the muddy fields of England. Well Ossie graced the game for many years and Ricky scored one of the best goals ever scored in a Wembley Final. The fact that this was after he had been substituted in the previous match and that it was the winning goal just added to the drama.

Ossie reigned in the middle of the field, avoiding tackles and knitting together defence and attack and knitting is exactly what he did. Skipping through the midfield, he either found or created a hole in the opposition's defence, as he weaved his way through it with the ball under close control. At just the right moment, he would release it, at the right weight, accurately, sometimes to run on and take the return and, at others, to enable one of his team mates to wreak the maximum damage. One opposition player is reputed to have said that tackling Ossie was like tackling dust. It couldn't have been better put by Shakespeare and, in addition, if true, shows that not all footballers are ignorant oafs. Some of them can even colour picture books in without going over the edges of the page.

Slight he may have been, ineffective he was not. In his two spells at the club, interrupted by the war with Argentina when he was loaned out to Paris St Germain, he made a total of 311 appearances scoring 25 goals. The technology to monitor a player's performance in terms of goals, assists, distance covered, etc. was not available in those days. However, I suspect that there was no one with a greater assists record. I don't know about distance although he seemed to cover a lot of that too.

An abiding memory of him comes from watching Spurs play Manchester United in the FA Cup in January 1980. After being held to 1-1 draw at home, the team travelled to Old Trafford where, in front of 53,762 fans, they won 1-0 with a goal from Ossie. I seem to remember that he stayed on the pitch afterwards, just looking around Old Trafford relishing the occasion. Not many teams knocked United out of the FA Cup on their own ground and he was going to enjoy every minute of it.

Ossie broke a leg in 1982 but continued to play for Spurs until 1988 when he was transferred to Blackburn Rover, then QPR and Swindon playing only 15 games total for all three clubs before becoming manager of the last of these in July 1989. Following spells with Newcastle and West Brom,

Ossie returned to manage Spurs under the chairmanship of Alan Sugar, as he was then. It was not, unfortunately, to be a glorious homecoming and, despite getting the team to play some thrilling attacking football, following a run of bad results, he was sacked in October 1994. I understand that even "You're fired" Sir Alan Sugar, found that difficult.

Ossie, along with Ricky Villa, was inducted into the Spurs Hall of Fame in February 2008 and deservedly so. Ricky is back home in Argentina, Ossie continued in management and now runs his own football school.

Glenn Hoddle

What can you say about Glenn other than he was one of the most cultured passers of a ball ever seen in the English game. In any other country, they would have built an international team around him and played to his strengths. Not, unfortunately, in England. Somewhere I read that even Ron Greenwood made some adverse comment when Glenn, prior to taking a free kick, kicked the toes of his boot into the ground to make sure that, like a golfer, he could putt the ball properly. Michel Platini, no mean player in his own right, although no great Anglophile where football is concerned, said that had Glenn Hoddle been born in France, he would have collected 150 caps. Monaco's captain at the time Glenn played there, Jean-Luc Ettori said, "For us Glenn was "le bon dieu", he was god, there is nothing else to say".

Arsene Wenger, his manager at Monaco, said that Glenn had perfect balance with superb control as well as skill in both feet. He went on to say that he couldn't understand why he hadn't been appreciated in his home country. "Perhaps he was a star in the wrong period, years ahead of his time". Some would even argue that he had greater public recognition at home in 1987 with the top 20 hit "Diamond Lights" with Chris Waddle. Those of us who prefer to remember the footballer like to gloss over that particular incident and the mullet hairstyle that went with it.

Recommended to Spurs by Martin Chivers, Glenn Hoddle finally signed in April 1974. After appearing for the England Youth team, he made his debut for Spurs, as a substitute, at home to Norwich City on 30 August 1975. Spurs could only manage a draw with goals from Pratt and Duncan. Glenn was just 17. Later that season, though, he made a real impact when in February 1976, he took the field from the start of the match at the Potteries against Stoke City. Spurs won 2-1 and Glenn scored the first goal with a great shot past Peter Shilton.

A possibly somewhat unheralded manager, Keith Burkinshaw, helped Glenn to thrive and, following relegation in 1976/7, in a young Spurs team, the playmaker helped them back to where they belonged, winning promotion at the first attempt. I remember listening to the football results on the radio at the Windscale demonstration in Trafalgar Square and knew that Spurs had to avoid defeat away to Southampton. They did with a 0-0 draw.

The following season saw him make 41 appearances scoring 19 goals. It was the season that he won the Professional Footballers' Association "Young Player of the Year" Award. He also made his international debut against Bulgaria scoring one of the goals in a 2-0 win.

During the following eight years, he would help Spurs to win the FA Cup (for the sixth time) against Manchester City in 1981, memorable for that Ricky Villa goal. The following season, they went on to retain the Cup, after a replay, with Glenn scoring in both matches. Perhaps a real tribute came, in October 1983, at the end UEFA Cup against a Feyenoord, with Johann Cruyff in the team. Spurs won 6-2 and, such was Glenn's performance, that after the match, the Dutchman went to the opposing dressing room and offered his shirt as a sign of respect.

Despite missing the match through worries over his fitness, he had been instrumental in getting the club to the UEFA Cup final in 1984, which they won. The 1987 Cup Final against Coventry, the only time that they had been beaten in the final of the competition, was his last for the club. At the end of the season, he signed for Monaco, newly managed by one Arsene Wenger. Sad though it was at the time, he left a legacy having played in 490 first team matches scoring 110 goals, a record of appearances bettered only by Perryman, Jennings, Mabbutt and Knowles. During this time, he also won 44 international caps.

At Monaco he helped the club to its first league title in six years. He went on to win the "Best Foreign Player in French Football" award but retired, though injury, in December 1990, at the age of 33. He continued his football career in management with, among others, Swindon, Spurs and England. In 2007, he was inducted into the National Football Museum Hall of Fame with a citation that reads "the most gifted English footballer of his generation exhibiting sublime balance and close control, unrivalled passing and vision and extraordinary shooting ability, both from open play and set pieces". Not a bad accolade that.

Richard Gough

For a player who only stayed a short while, Richard Gough made a real impression on me. An uncompromising though cultured centre half in a combination that you didn't often see in those days, he could be described as a cross between Alderweireld and Vertonghen. He was a great tackler, commanding in the air and could distribute the ball well once he'd won it. His authority as a player epitomised in his calmness under pressure and his confidence in all he did made him a natural leader and captain, a position he occupied at Dundee, Tottenham, Rangers and Scotland.

Born in 1962, he grew up in South Africa coming to the UK to become a professional footballer. After signing for Charlton Athletic, a club his father played for, he was eventually snapped up by Dundee United at the age of 18. After six seasons he signed for Spurs for about £750,000 but stayed little over a year and captained the team in their one FA Cup Final defeat against Coventry City. Graham Souness, as manager of Rangers, took him back to Scotland where he enjoyed enormous success captaining the Rangers side that went on to win nine consecutive league titles.

After playing in the US he returned to England to resume his football career with, among others, Everton, another team schooled in the game's finer arts, before retiring at the age of 40. He left me and other Spurs' fans with memories of that quiet authority that we witnessed for such a short time. Had Grahame Souness not persuaded Spurs to let him leave, the history of the club and its achievements would, in my view, have been somewhat better that they were in subsequent years. As so often with Tottenham, it was a case of what might have been.

Paul Gascoigne

Paul Gascoigne was a talent so outrageous that it is a wonder that it could be contained in one body and, maybe, there lies part of his problem. There is a story that, when he arrived at Spurs, in one training session he took the ball round most of those on the pitch, including the goalie, to score. The players are reputed to have stood and applauded. I can believe that to be true and hope that it is. Gascoigne had a combination of skills which added up to something very, very special. He had vision in the way that Glenn Hoddle did and could pass a ball with accuracy over distance. He could dribble past opponents as if they didn't exist and he had a shot that was unerringly accurate and could be delivered with power. Witness that free kick against Arsenal in the FA Cup semi final of 1991.

Unfortunately the man/boy that was Paul Gascoigne could be somewhat reckless and that certainly helped curtail his career. Pumped up in the Cup Final, his first tackle on Garry Parker was at chest level and probably merited a red card on its own. Soon afterwards, however, in the 13th minute, he committed another reckless tackle on Gary Charles. He was stretchered of with damaged knee ligaments and never played for Spurs again. By the time he had recovered, he was with Lazio where Dino Zoff would say that he was one of the nicest players he'd ever met. I think those seasons at Spurs showed some of the best of him. It could have continued for so much longer but, as with all else with Gazza and Spurs, it was not to be. More's the pity as he may well have been the most naturally gifted footballer ever to play for England and that's saying something.

Teddy Sheringham

Teddy was a footballing brain on legs and not the fastest legs at that. A hard, tough player but an incredibly skilful one who made the ball do the work. Said by Jurgen Klinsman to be the most intelligent strike partner he ever played with, he really was that good. Arriving at Spurs via Millwall and Nottingham Forest, he was signed by Terry Venables, no mean judge of a footballer, in 1992 for £2.1m.

If you read the internet, you will see that he is described, perhaps with some humour, as "a retired English footballer and the father of Charlie Sheringham". He played as a striker and had a successful career at club level winning almost every domestic honour, most notably the treble with Manchester United; the pinnacle of this career probably in scoring one goal and setting up the other in the final minutes of the European Cup Final 0f 1998/9. He was awarded the OBE in 2007 and retired from competitive football in 2007/8 at the age of 42. As a précis of a career, it's not bad. As a description, it leaves a lot to be desired.

Although he could hold the ball up well, the football flowed when Teddy played. He was champagne on the pitch. Watch the England v Holland game in the 1996 European Championships when England won 4-1 or the last 20 minutes of that European Cup Final. In the latter, impatient to get on (and probably annoyed that he hadn't been on the pitch earlier), you knew just what he was going to do and he did it. The story is that it was so late in the game, that the Bayern Munich ribbons had already been tied to the trophy. A bit premature with Sheringham playing in what was probably his last chance to win such a prize.

Another player who graced the game and left fond memories with the fans of most of the clubs he played for and harsh ones for the centre halves he played against. Not a bad record that.

Jurgen Klinsmann

"The Diver" before he came to Spurs. He played for the club in two seasons, 1994/5 and 1997/8. When he first arrived in England, like many others, I wasn't keen. He was a diver and yet, within a short time he had achieved cult status and left, for Bayern Munich, a hero, with the Football Writers' Association Player of the Year Award. One writer in The Guardian, having written an article "Why I Hate Jurgen Klinsman" followed it some months later with another, "Why I Love Jurgen Klinsman". Perhaps the start helped when, having scored, he dived in celebration and the fans took him as one of their own. He returned a second time to save the club from relegation.

When he first signed, Ossie was still the manager. Jurgen's 29 goals helped the club get to seventh in the league and, under the new manager Gerry Francis, reach the semi finals of the FA Cup before going out to Everton. It was a slightly different set of circumstances when he returned in December of 1997. Under the London Underground ticket wielding Christian Gross, Spurs were in a relegation struggle. In the last game but one, away to Wimbledon, no easy ground to get a result at, Jurgen notched up four goals in a 6-2 win. At home to Southampton for the final game and they could only draw 1-1. Guess who scored the Spurs goal? Jurgen left the club, probably in his beloved Beetle to play for his country in the World Cup, after which he retired. He changed a nation's views playing with style and no little skill. Thanks, Jurgen. Come back any time.

David Ginola

Reportedly called a freak by David Pleat, that is exactly
what he was. Fast, unbelievably skilful, two footed, he was
El Magnifico. Watch his goals on the internet and wonder
what might have been in a better team than, probably, any
of those he played for. Even women who don't like football
could get the idea when watching him. Then again he was
extremely good looking and, dare I say it, French.

David was a one off even for a left winger, a difficult
position for a club to fill. As a player, he didn't ghost past
defenders but ignored them; they may have been there but
he had better things to do that waste his time taking any
notice of them. His touch was sure, his dribbling, mesmeric
and his shooting, powerful. Look on the internet for one
match for Spurs where the ball was cleared by an opposing
defender. Unfortunately for the opposition, 20 yards out, it
fell to David. On the volley, he struck it beautifully and it
was in the back of the next before anyone moved. He ran
off waving his hand as if it was scorched, an appropriate
gesture. Another, I think, in an FA Cup match where he
weaved his way through the opposing defence to slot the ball
in the net with some style. That's what he had, style. He was
a natural for Spurs until George Graham can along and he
was sold to Aston Villa. Bloody barmy for a man who, in
1999, was said by Johan Cruyff to be the best player in the
world.

David, I'm sorry that your skills never graced the teams
they should have and that you are not available to play anymore for Tottenham. Rest, safe in the knowledge that Spurs
and Newcastle fans consider themselves lucky to have seen
you strut your stuff. Bugger the mere mortals of the world,
they can play for other clubs.

Dimitar Berbatov

It will probably make me unpopular among some of my fellow supporters but I do think Berbatov was one of the most unbelievable footballers I've ever seen. Mesmeric, sublime and consumately skilful, he was capable of making your jaw drop to the floor with moments that took your breath away. Some touches and movements that you simply did not believe had happened. You had just seen them, as had 40,000 other people, and yet you couldn't quite believe the evidence of your own eyes. Whether it was calmly, with his outstretched leg at chest height, pulling a hoofed ball from the goalie down as if it was glued to his boot and, in one movement beating a defender or, as against Charlton, on the left wing flicking the ball on, from a long pass from Ledley King. In one movement, he was past the defender running 30 yards to beat the opposition goalie and score. Only three people had touched the ball and the match was, effectively, over. Down to ten men at home against Bolton, often Spurs' bogey team at that time, he gave a one man display up front that many have never seen bettered. Yes he didn't tackle back. Yes he behaved badly over his move to Manchester United. Yes he was moody. Yes, he did not find it easy at Old Trafford, but what a player. He's on my list.

Luka Modric

With the ball at his feet, skipping, swaying and flowing, Luka Modric was poetry in motion. Not particularly tall or powerfully built, he could still look after himself in the battleground that is the middle of a football pitch. He played for Spurs for just 4 seasons from 2008/2012. I could provide you with all the details of goals, matches played, etc but will concentrate on the player himself; recently described as the best all round midfielder in the world. It's a description I find it difficult to disagree with.

Even at 31, he still bears a startling resemblance to a young boy. Yet to see him play is to witness an aggressiveness that belies his slightness of frame. Once the results of that quality have been carved out, his more elegant skills assert themselves. So much so that he is able to dictate the play and set the rhythm of the game with them. Instant control, always the mark of a quality footballer, the ability to keep possession when others are intent on ensuring that you don't and that distinctive swaying run. Neat, precise, short passes that weave patterns in the middle of the pitch and build up to an attack or those long sweeping ones that take out half the opposition in one move; Luka has it all. In his way, he is the heart of the team and one that is sadly missed by this supporter.

Gareth Bale

As a young player, Gareth seemed to be drifting away from Spurs as yet another prodigy who never quite made it. Well, this one was a prodigy who did make it, in abundance; both at Spurs and Real Madrid. A product of Southampton's Academy, who had identified him as young as nine years of age, he nearly went to Old Trafford. It seems that Fergie didn't offer quite enough and Spurs jumped in and signed him in May 2007. Well done, that man, whoever he was; this one is sheer class. Fit as a butcher's dog and built like Adonis, he is left footed, can run all day at speed with the ball under his control, cross, head the ball, hit a mean dead ball and score. Moreover, he seems to be a very down to earth young man. If the story is correct, he was once told by Harry Redknapp to take a couple of days off. The instruction seems to have been, get a holiday. The popular image would have been of a footballer jetting off to the sun with a young lady in tow. Gareth, reportedly, went home to see his mum.

Even though he scored quite early in his Spurs' career, he had to undergo surgery and then went 24 games without being on a winning Premiership side. When Benoit Assou-Ekotto was sidelined with injury, Gareth got his opportunity and, boy, did he grasp it with both hands? The result is that the following seasons saw seen him develop into, literally, a world class player. Not nippy and speedy but, more like a Rolls Royce with that silent, unbelievably powerful acceleration that you hardly noticed until you saw the opposing defender trailing in his wake. Ask Maicon Douglas Sisenando, otherwise previously known as the best full back in the world. Until he came up against young Gareth, that is. It appears that, after Gareth scored a hat trick, Spurs' fans were shouting, "Taxi for Mr Maicon". Mind you, the team were 4 – 0 down at the time. Typical Tottenham. Unfortunately, Spurs couldn't hold onto him and he was transferred to Real Madrid as the most expensive footballer in the world. After a difficult start he has flourished and, on the international stage, drove Wales into the semi final of the European Championship 2016. Moreover he is still in his prime. I'm just glad that, albeit on television, I watched him play; one of a trio of my all time greats who have all occupied the left wing.

Ledley King

But for his knees, Ledley King may well have been the best centre half Spurs had during the whole time I've watched them. Now retired due to his injuries, he was the longest serving player at the club at the time. Calm, authoritative, dependable, fast and solid in the air and on the ground with excellent timing, he had everything. So much so that Thierry Henri is reported to have said that, when Ledley tackled you, you didn't even realise you'd been tackled. You just noticed that you didn't have the ball at your feet anymore. What a way of describing his ability. Henri also described him as the best defender in Europe and the only one in the Premiership who could regularly tackle him without committing a foul.

Just imagine what the Tottenham defence might have been like had he been able to play regularly. Instead Ledley only reached his 200th league game in October 2008, nine years after his debut. Despite this paucity of appearances, The Times newspaper named him as the 25th best Tottenham player of all time.

As someone who watched him, you couldn't help but notice that he often played an understated game, quietly getting on with his job. Indeed you often noticed him more by his absence, with the resultant increase in the goals against figures, than you did by his presence. I really like that in a person. Team captain for four years, he remained the club captain until his retirement. I know that it may not mean too much but it does demonstrate the esteem in which he is held. Unfortunately, there was no effective treatment for the knee problems he had yet, in his final season and unable to train, he still played 23 times for the club. Remarkably, in his whole career, he only received 8 yellow cars, something of a record for a defender. Harry Redknapp called him a freak for being able to play at the level he did without training. Martin Jol thought that he was the best central defender he had ever seen. Some accolade that. Talking of the best, however, takes me neatly onto the player I regard as simply "The Best".

One Very Special Player

Unfortunately not Tottenham player. However, no book on English football would be complete without a mention of George Best. Was there ever a more appropriately named player? In my view, there wasn't and probably never will be unless someone names their child "George (or whatever), greatest footballing genius ever to have lived, Best", because that's what he was. Simply the best. However, before I begin my eulogy to the greatest player ever to come out of these islands to date, I would like to add some sort of context, probably to do with my age.

As you get older, people you knew or knew of, well known people, relatives and friends, die. Life, unfortunately, is like that. It necessarily ends in death. My normal reaction, especially when it happens to famous people, is a quiet acknowledgment to myself of their passing followed by getting on with whatever I'm doing. George's death was different and, even now, some years after it happened, it is still difficult to take in. I can see nothing other than that slim, graceful, good looking genius weaving his way around a football pitch and his opponents. It is still a very clear picture in my mind. Probably because he looks like a skinny boy, with his socks rolled down, enjoying himself without a thought in his head other than running around with a football at his feet.

For those who never saw him play, probably the majority of football lovers today, he is a figure from the past, which he is. However, he really was a being from another universe such was the unbelievable natural ability he displayed. It's as if the gods decided that they would send down someone who could show the human race, at least that part of it that watches the game, just how it was meant to be played and, boy, did he do just that? In match after match, at the highest level, he plied his trade leaving the opposition trailing in his wake. Not for nothing was the saying in his native country, "Maradona, good, Pele, better, George Best".

If you get the opportunity, watch a clip from a match between Manchester United and Chelsea when George is tackled by Ron Harris, "Chopper" to his friends. His enemies didn't call him anything as they probably spent their time picking bits of his boot out of where their teeth had been. On a pitch that left something to be desired, it shows George, with the ball at his feet weaving through the mud towards the penalty area. Chopper comes in from one side and slightly behind at ankle level, like a lorry load of bricks being delivered at 80 mile an hour. Even though the tackle seems to catch him, George somehow keeps his balance leaving Chopper on the floor in his wake, an achievement in itself. He then holds off the attention of two other defenders and rounds Peter Bonnetti to put the ball into the back of the net. I heard somewhere that he considered it his best ever goal. How could he tell when there were so many?

One on the internet, however, is recorded as his best. In the North American Soccer League in 1981 when he was way past his prime. Watch the defenders, five in all, running around like headless chickens who haven't a clue how to deal with him as he weaves his way through the penalty area before left footing the ball into the net. One defender is supposed to have had to have an operation after marking George; to untie the knots that his spine was in.

He played for United, firstly under Sir Matt Busby, in a line up that included himself, Dennis Law and Bobbie Charlton, a trio that has, probably, never been bettered. He faced the toughest of defenders who had one aim in mind, to stop him at all costs. Mostly, they didn't. Yet, after 11 years in the first team from 1963 until 1974 and after numerous problems related to enjoying himself off the pitch, he walked out of United at the age of 27.

Many years later when I was married again and settled down, my wife, Gaynor, and I went for a drink with her brother and his wife in the Fiennes Arms and there he was sitting on his own. As someone who does his best to ignore celebrities, I was awestruck. It seemed rude to disturb him and I didn't. I do remember that he paid for his drink from a large roll of notes.

"Where did it all go wrong?" was the question often asked of him and it was a valid one, reinforced by the quote from Michael Parkinson below. George, I understand, used to use it in his after dinner speeches. He described being in a hotel room with one of the Miss World's he dated with a deal of money that he'd just won spread out on the bed. A waiter brought up some drinks and, as he left, is quoted as asking the question. George's response was something along the lines that "All this is going wrong?" Another, oft quoted comment was, "I spent a lot of money on booze, birds and fast cars. The rest I squandered". Given the life he led, his early death at 59 was understandable, yet I can only see that slim boy weaving his way past defenders thoroughly enjoying himself. It will remain with me forever and that is some legacy. I finish with some reported quotes by or about George.

"I used to go missing a lot, Miss Canada, Miss United Kingdom, Miss World".

"In 1969 I gave up women and alcohol. It was the worst 20 minutes of my life."

Following a liver transplant in 2002, "I was in for 10 hours and had 40 pints, beating my previous record by 20 minutes."

"They say I slept with seven Miss Worlds but I didn't. It was only four. I didn't turn up for the other three".

From TV presenter and friend, Sir Michael Parkinson, "The only tragedy George Best had to confront is that he will never know how good he could have been".

Added to his signature on a ball given to George as a tribute, from Pele, "From the second best player in the world".

The telegram sent to Sir Matt Busby by Bob Bishop after he discovered Best playing for Cregagh Boys' Club, aged 15 said "Boss, I think I've found you a genius". He had.

Legends

Legends are not necessarily the greatest players, instead they are just legends, remembered for a number of reasons, commitment and effort being among them. Some attain legendary status for unidentifiable reasons other than you can feel their passion for the club. Simply, you get to like them. As with the list of my greatest players, any list of legends will be agreed and disagreed with. They also, as with the great players, include only those I have seen live or on television fairly regularly. The list includes the great players, minus Dimitar Berbatov, plus:

Gary Mabbut

Gary Mabbut is probably top of my list although it is a close run thing between him and Steve Perryman. Gary was Spurs through and through, even turning down, it is said, a transfer to Liverpool at their best, to stay at the club. A diabetic who wrote to a number of clubs, most of whom were not interested, presumably because of the diabetes, he got taken on at Spurs. It proved to be one of their better signings. He was Mr Dependable but not in the slightly negative sense in which that term is sometimes used.

You really could depend on him. There was also something else which I have never been able to put my finger on and am still struggling now. He had some sort of honesty and decency in the way he played that filtered through and reflected itself on the terraces who took him as one of their own. An acceptance and liking for him as a person that is the mark of a club legend.

He served the club for 16 years, from 1982 until 1998, as a defensive midfielder but with great all round ability. This was shown when, despite the fact that he was not particularly tall, he had an ability to out jump many of the taller strikers he faced which led to him sometimes being played at centre half. He was the anchor around which the team grounded, a role that led him to being appointed team captain and he played like you would expect a captain to play, leading by example.

Given his position in the team, you would expect Gary to have had his fair share of injuries, which he did. The worst by far was from one of John Fashanu's elbows in 1993/4, Fash the Bash, as he was known. The injury fractured Gary's cheekbone and his eye socket in a number of places and he returned, with a metal plate inserted, the following season. He also became somewhat of an icon for those with diabetes, especially children, appearing on Blue Peter where he showed, using an orange, how he had to inject himself every day. Gary is also famous in Coventry where the club's fanzine is known as "Gary Mabbut's Knee" after the own goal he scored in the 1987 Cup Final. A game Coventry won when Spurs lost their 100% record in finals. Interestingly, I don't think anyone at Spurs thinks it was Gary's fault.

He also helped Spurs to win the UEFA Cup in 1984 and the FA Cup, against Nottingham Forest, as captain, in 1991. He also made 16 appearances for his country scoring against Yugoslavia in 1986. Unfortunately, he broke a leg on the opening day of the 1996/7 campaign and was out for the whole season. By the time he retired at 37, he was the club's longest serving player, with 618 games and 36 goals for the club. An inspiration showing how you can succeed at the highest level despite what others would consider a disabling illness.

Steve Perryman

Another Mr Dependable, Steve made his league debut at the age of 17 and became team captain at the age of just 20 going on to make a record 854 first team appearances between 1969 and 1986. He still holds the club record for most appearances in the league, F.A. Cup, League Cup and Europe. In a long, successful career Steve also won more medals than any other player at Spurs with two League Cups, two UEFA Cups and two F.A. Cups alongside the honour of the Football Writers' Player of the Year in 1982. A midfielder, he scored 89 goals and was voted the Football Writers' Association Footballer of the Year in 1982. In his time at the club he helped them to win the UEFA Cup in 1972 and 1984, the FA Cup in 1981 and 1982 and the League Cup in 1971 and 1973. Steve is currently Director of Football at Exeter City FC.

Graham Roberts

Had he followed a career in films, Graham Roberts would have been the stuntman who walked through brick walls for the star. And walk through walls he did. Well, actually, he demolished them taking the ball (fairlyish), the player, those in the opposing team who happened to be in the way, the goalposts and netting and half the front row of the stands in the process. It's a wonder that they didn't all finish in the High Road. He literally gave 100% and, in doing so, encouraged others to do the same. Not for nothing is his autobiography entitled "Hard as Nails". Dave Mackay's heir.

Ricky Villa

If for nothing else, Ricky is a legend for that goal at Wembley in the 100th FA Cup final. Buccaneering looks and a footballing style to match, he had thighs like tree trunks, ploughing through the muddy pitches of England as if there dry ground. A bit of a colossus that one.

Cyril Knowles RIP

Most of us get a reasonable time span on this earth. Others, mainly rock stars, are like comets, they shine brightly for a short time before burning up. Jim Morrison, Janis Joplin. Jimi Hendrix, Keith Moon and Brian Jones, to name but a few. Fame can certainly consume people, especially those who are, for whatever reason, somewhat fragile. It doesn't often seem to happen to footballers. Their careers may be shortened by injury, their lives, not. Cyril Knowles was one of the exceptions.

Born in Fitzwilliam in Yorkshire, Cyril started his career in the position that he graced for many years, left back. While playing for his local team, he was rejected by, among others, Manchester United. Middlesbrough, however, signed him and he made his first team debut there in 1962/3. After only 39 first team appearances, Bill Nicholson signed him towards the end of the following season as a replacement for Ron Henry. He made his first team debut, along with Pat Jennings, on the opening day of the following season at White Hart Lane where Spurs beat Sheffield United 2-0 with goals from Jimmy Greaves and Frank Saul. A healthy 45,112 watched the match and the start of the career of a player who some regard as the best left back ever to play for the club.

Renowned for his play as an overlapping full back and his accurate crossing ability, Cyril could also defend. He became a firm favourite with the fans and remained that way throughout the whole of his 11 years with the club. His partnership with a young (and very slim) Joe Kinnear gave Spurs great full back coverage which, along with Alan Mullery and, later, Mike England gave the team a defensive solidity they are, only now, surpassing. Hence that long run of games without defeat in 1966/7.

In all, Cyril played 507 games for the club scoring 17 goals and ensuring that a great many more were prevented. He helped the club win the FA Cup in 1967, the League Cup twice, in 1971 and 1973 and the UEFA Cup in 1972. After a series of persistent knee injuries, at 31 in December 1975, he played his last competitive game for the club in a 2-2 home draw against Everton, ending a glorious career. By contrast, Cyril experienced tragedy is his personal life. Driving one day with his young son in the passenger seat, a stone was thrown up and through the windscreen. It hit Cyril's son of the forehead and he died. In February 1991, Cyril was diagnosed with a brain tumour and he died in August of that year aged 47.

Among those who don't follow football, Cyril is probably best remembered in the catch phrase, "Nice one, Cyril" in a popular song which reached number 14 in the Hit Parade in 1973. It is rumoured that Cyril didn't like the song one bit.

Michael Dawson

There's also one other player that I'd like to give a mention to and that's Michael Dawson. Purchased, along with Andy Reid, from Nottingham Forest, he was a centre half who gave his all for the club. With Michael, you got what it said on the tin and, for me, it was a sad day when he left the club. Hearing him being interviewed, it was obvious where his allegiances lay and they were with Spurs through and through. So, after nine glorious years, he was transferred to Hull and now plays his football in the Championship; unless another club want a truly committed player of no little ability.

Interestingly, in the season that his transfer to Spurs took place, I was doing some work with the local authority whose offices were next door to the City ground where Forest played. When I visited, I used to pop into the local newsagent to get a newspaper and the shopkeeper and I got talking about football. When I told him that I was a Spurs' supporter, he told me that the players the club had just bought were the two best that Forest had. Being a forward of no little skill, I was taken by Andy Reid only to have him tell me that, Michael Dawson was in a different class. Given, the resultant performances and longevity at Spurs, he was right.

.

The Next Generation

Now I'm fully cognisant of the fact that, in writing this section, I'm making myself a hostage to fortune. However, it would be remiss of me not to write about those who could well be the future great Spurs' players and, even, legends. It goes almost without saying that the overall quality of the current squad is, probably, as good as any that I've seen at White Hart Lane; which makes the task even more difficult. Also, this group plays more as a team than, probably any other that I've watched. So, perhaps, it would be easier to include them all, which I could well do in truth. How do you select from among this current crop of young players?

Well, forcing myself to make a judgement, I've opted for those who have already demonstrated their qualities consistently, at the highest level above those who, whatever the circumstances, have done that less so. So, my list doesn't include a likely future captain of his country in Eric Dier, one who has improved, probably, more than any other in Danny Rose and midfield maestro that is Christian Eriksen.

Like the other lists, this, short one, will be disputed and, in my view, it comes down to four players, Harry Kane,

Mousa Dembele, Deli Ali and Victor Wanyama.

Harry is a deceptive player but one who has it all. Raised on all those homegrown strikers of the past who were, shall we say, OK, it took me a while to see Harry as the real deal. This despite his record; I must have been blind. It's almost as if he crept up without too many people noticing; or maybe that was just me. Not especially powerfully built, he is a player who is extremely difficult to get off the ball. He can score with his head and both feet and, it has to be said, is absolutely tireless for the team. He is probably the archetypical Pochettino player. Moreover, he seems to delight in scoring against our north London rivals. He's also only 24 and should have his best years in front of him. What's not to like?

If it's difficult to get the ball off Harry, it's impossible to get it off Mousa Dembele. Immensely strong but, for a big man, surprisingly balletic, he can glide past opposing defenders with ease and arrive in the danger area, seemingly with little effort and the ball still glued to his foot. When he does let loose towards goal, he has a powerful shot and there's my only criticism; he doesn't do that often enough. Mind you, it seems that he has often played through injury so maybe we haven't always seen what he's really capable of. If that is the case, then the future can only be better.

Like Harry, in his position, Delli Ali has it all. Mind you, if quotes from the manager are to be believed, that's not just in his current position. As a player, he seems to arrive, unnoticed, in just the right place at the right time and in much the same way that Martin Peters did. Witness his two headed goals, from virtually the same position, against Chelsea last season. You'd have thought that, after the first one, that team of seasoned warriors would have noticed but, no. So why do it once when you can do it twice? Which is precisely what he did.

He can glide past defenders, is incredibly sharp and good with feet and head. Moreover, he's no pushover and will let those, more seasoned, players know that he's on the pitch; a useful quality for a young 'un who wants to impose himself on the battle ground that is the midfield. In addition, his goal tally is incredible for a midfielder. Indeed, it seems that he's already scored more goals than both Steven Gerard and Frank Lampard at a similar age. Not bad when you consider their records. One of those players for whom the world is his oyster.

Victor Wanyama is the sort of player that Spurs have needed almost for as long as I can remember. Mind you, I do have a shorter memory these days. In reality, the last time I saw a defensive midfielder of his ilk, was in the days of Alan Mullery, Gary Mabbut, Graham Roberts and Steve Perryman. Imperious though he may seem at times, his real forte is simply in ensuring that "thus far and no further", at least with the ball, is the order of the day for those among the opposition. Helped in this by a stance that is upright and a build that is intimidating, he also has the ability to help set up the next attack. He can, on occasion, even double up as a centre half. Thanks, Victor, for making me feel that I haven't been wasting my breath all these years.

The Ones
Who Got Away,
the Expensive,
the Not So Good
and the Wasted

The trouble with football is that, as a mere supporter, you may never know who most of these were, the transfer market being a hotbed of rumour, misinformation and just plain lies. So it's probably best to stick with those who, it is common knowledge, could have joined Spurs and the difference they might have made. Two, at least, spring to mind, Johnny Haynes and Jim Baxter. Both wonderfully skilled midfielders with artistry that could change a game in an instant. In their different ways, also characters.

I saw Baxter play for Sunderland during the season that it had been anticipated that he would move to White Hart Lane. It was an evening match at Tottenham under floodlight and he strolled onto the pitch as if he owned it. Tall, dark, slim and graceful, the man who God took his instructions from, had descended into N17 and blessed us with his presence, albeit for a very short while. The floodlights against the dark sky emphasising the sacredness of the occasion. Slim Jim knew how good he was and so did we. His sense of occasion was sublime and he set about demonstrating just what we'd missed so that, even if we didn't know it before, we certainly would after that night. Unfortunately God's superior was surrounded that night by mere mortals who were not of the same species, at least on the Sunderland side.

Alex Ferguson allegedly described Slim Jim as "Arguably the best player to play in Scottish football and the greatest player I ever played with. He had touch, balance, vision and just this wonderful aura." On that night he sprayed passes that were inch perfect over the length of half the pitch, delivered after a sway of the hips that sent the poor sod marking him the wrong way. Nothing played at other than the pace that he dictated and that pace with little regard for those lesser mortals who feel that football is about running. Jim let his feet and the ball do the work allied to a football brain that was second to none at the time.

No one who ever saw him in his pomp would disagree with the Manchester United manager's assessment. Unfortunately Jim liked a drink, eventually having two liver transplants and dying at the age of 55. No matter, for a short while, a young man on a dark floodlit night at White Hart Lane saw a vision that remains with him to this day. Thank you, Slim Jim, for showing me that dreams don't have to be just dreams. For an hour and a half that night, you made them come true.

Johnny Haynes was a one club player and that club was Fulham; unfortunately for Spurs who wanted to buy him during Bill Nicholson's management. Playing a record 658 games for the club, "The Maestro" was described by Pele as the best passer of the ball that he had ever seen. While Jim Baxter was one of the new breed of footballers in his attitude, Johnny Haynes was very much old school albeit one who personally led the way for the new contingent when he became the first £100 a week footballer in 1961. Hard though it may be to believe today, until then footballers were restricted to a wage of £20 per week. The story is that the then club chairman and famous comedian, Tommy Trinder, had stated that Haynes was worth £100 per week, not expecting the £20 ceiling to be removed. When it was, he is supposed to have paid up without comment, although in Tommy Trinder's case, that is hard to believe; he was never short of a comment.

Not regarded as a great goalscorer, he still managed 158 for the club and 18 for England in 56 internationals, 22 of them as captain. A member of both the 1958 and 1962 World Cup squads, he is remembered for being the mastermind behind a winning sequence between 1960 and 1961 in which England scored 40 goals in six matches.

Once the subject of a major bid from Spurs, he was wanted by Bill Nicholson to provide the ammunition for Jimmy Greaves. The friendship between the two players demonstrated when Fulham played at White Hart Lane. It was a long time ago but I seem to remember a fracas in the penalty area which the referee took a while to resolve. During this time Jimmy called Johnny Haynes over and they stood together, seeming, for all the world to be calmly discussing the weather. They played well together for England and who knows what they would have achieved together at Spurs. It was not to be and Johnny Haynes also got away.

If a player is good, they will justify the money spent on them. Hence they are not really, in my book, expensive. Expensive means that they cost an awful lot of money at the time and didn't succeed quite as they were expected to. And, at Spurs, there have been far too many of them over far too many years. When I first started writing this book, I listed some of these with the intention of their making the final cut. Unfortunately, they would have constituted a book in their own right. Besides, players have little say in the fee that is paid for them so it seems somewhat unfair to criticise them on that basis. Not that I haven't criticised some of them because I have. However, I've done this on the basis of their abilities or lack of them. Also there are some players, and I'm thinking here of the likes of Vincent Jansen, who the supporters often take a real liking to and will them to succeed. Not that that they always do.

Just as an example though, it's worth looking at the players that were brought in on the basis of Gareth Bale's move to Real Madrid during the summer of 2013. The, so called, "Magnificent 7" cost a reported total of almost £110m. Only two of them are now with the club with, despite Erik Lamela's undoubted skills, only Christian Eriksen being considered an unqualified success. Yet this pattern of buying established stars was standard procedure for Spurs (and many other clubs) for many years. Unfortunately it is one that has a high failure rate. Fortunately, by accident or design, it is one that Spurs are no longer adhering to with the club's emphasis on home grown talent.

There's a PhD thesis in there somewhere for any Spurs loving student. As such theses tend to be about obscure matters, you could entitle it, "The rational pursuit of perfection by irrational means, a story of football transfer dealings at the highest level in one particular club over a ten year period". It would be sufficiently obscure with a title sufficiently long for such dissertations and could well reach conclusions that would be equally obscure. As were the reasons that some of these players were bought.

The real questions that needs to be asked is that, in the small world that is professional football, did nobody warn the club of what they were buying, did the club not ask or close their ears to what they heard or what? Of course, there are alternatives related to that regular turnover of management at the club; among which are that a player who may have been good under one manager and style of play may not be so under another and is not given the chance to prove otherwise. Perhaps that is why managers, when they take over at a club, are prone to return to their previous clubs for players that they had already worked with.

I don't like the idea of labelling players as the worst so I am being diplomatic, not my strong suit, in saying that they were just not the best. There are, in football, players who seem to lack the necessary skills to perform the tasks that they had been employed to. Some may have been not so bad but were, maybe, at the wrong club or at the right club but at the wrong time. Some, to be honest were bad. The ones I remember, though, are those who scared the wits out of me every time they got the ball. Usually these were defenders.

You will all have your own and I have mine which, for the purposes of this book, I've limited to three. Yes, I know, not many given some of the players that the club has bought over the years. Still, if I was to list them all, there would be two main consequences. The first is that a great number of libel suits might be in the offing, unless I selected only players who were dead, while the second is that the book would be twice as long. So, these three are either defenders or midfielders all bought within the time that I've supported the club; so that gives anyone scope for conjecture.

The first of these scared me every time he had the ball. No one knew what he was going to do when he got it, not even the player himself. I remember once watching him on the right side of defence in or near the penalty area. All arms and raised legs, he could have been someone who had wandered off Hackney Marshes, asked for a game and been amazed when he had found himself on the pitch, let alone in the first team. Even just bloody hoofing it half way up the field would have helped but, seemingly with no idea, he appeared to want to play football. A defender in his own, crowded, penalty area. Eddie the Eagle in football boots except that Eddie tried to master his sport. This player didn't seem to understand how to play the game. I won't say he didn't try just that he'd have been better off not doing so. I don't think I have ever been so relieved to see a player leave. The question, however, was "Why was he bought?"

The second was a centre half, a problem area for Spurs for many years. This one also a trier who didn't inspire confidence. Also remembered as an "arms and legs" player, he was in the team that drew 5-5 with Aston Villa in April 1966 after being 5-1 up at half time. It gets worse; had, Alan Mullery, I think, not cleared the ball off the line at the end of the match, Villa would have won 5-6. Their centre forward that day was one Tony Hateley and he scored four times. Although, the player had opened the scoring for Spurs which may well have contributed to his downfall. Perhaps that went to his head because, from then on, the ball never did. The next time I remember seeing a match quite like that was in the FA against Manchester City which is described in another chapter.

The last is a midfielder, still with the club. Quite why he was purchased, for what is seems to be a rather large fee, is anyone's guess.

Of all the top clubs, Spurs probably hold the record for buying, seemingly, talented players only to see them disappear, drift or whatever into football's wastelands. Or, maybe, that's just my perception and other clubs are as bad. Interestingly, in the two cases that I describe, the players are young ones that that the club appears to have spent some years tracking. Enter Wayne Routledge and John Bostock. The first of these followed an acrimonious transfer from Crystal Palace, a few minor turnouts for Spurs, some sort of injury, if I remember correctly, then he was off. You could argue that his career since has not been what had been anticipated at the time but that would miss the point. A few seasons ago, John Bostock, also from Crystal Palace, arrived amid so much acrimony that the Palace threatened to revoke the player and his stepfather's season ticket. When last heard of Bostock was plying his trade in Belgium.

Mind you, I now have to dramatically revise my thinking. The past few seasons, under Mauricio Pochettino, have seen a revolution at Tottenham. This, both in terms of their playing style and recruitment of players. There have, however, still been a number of howlers although, in recent years, more related to attacking players than defenders.

The Best Managers

What is it that actually makes a good football manager and why do there appear to be so few at the very top level of English football? Now, there really is a PhD subject!

In the past, these people were at the centre of the club and synonymous with it. They also tended not to take centre stage publicly too much, if at all. You can't imagine Bill Nicholson having a microphone shoved up his nose at half time and being questioned about the team's performance, can you? The very successful ones tend to be an extremely rare breed and, given the rate at which they are now being hired and fired by their employers, not many of the next generation of managers will get the opportunity to gain the experience necessary to become successful themselves. It may be easier just to pocket the compensation and retire. In fact, there might even be a money making scam here on the part of less competent but charismatic managers persuading boards of Directors to take them on before being found out, fired and paid off. At which point they move to another club and repeat the process. Does that particular merry go round sound familiar to anyone? So, before they all die out, I give you my choices as the best managers in the English game.

Sir Alex Ferguson

Football fans will argue forever over who is or was the best manager of all in English football. So I offer, as with the players, my humble view. First either Sir Alex Ferguson or Matt Busby. What they both did and, in the case of the former, until relatively recently was still doing, at Old Trafford can brook little argument. Not just the success on the field but the ability to mould a team of almost unrivalled talents and get them playing together with a high degree of consistency, week after week and to sustain that success over many years. Lots of managers manage lesser talents, managing the greater ones takes some doing and they did it for a combined total of 50 years.

If I have to choose, I would like to let my heart rule my head but somehow I find I can't. When push comes to shove and by a small margin, I think I will opt for the recent incumbent and say, "Arise, Sir Alex". What he did with Aberdeen in the eight years from 1978 until 1986 was remarkable. Unused to such success, the club won the league title in 1979/80 followed by three successive Scottish Cup wins from 1982 until 1984 with two more league titles in 1983/4 and 1984/5. The European Cup Winners' Cup against the mighty Real Madrid came in between in May 1983 with the European Super Cup Championship in December of that year. Finally in 1985/6, Aberdeen won the Scottish Cup and the League Cup before the manager left for Manchester United. Reportedly, having turned Tottenham down in the meantime.

He didn't have a great start at Old Trafford after taking over from Ron Atkinson in November 1986. Yet, seemingly with his job threatened, the team won the FA Cup in 1989 and he went on to build and rebuild, probably five teams in 26 years, each one, seemingly, better than the last. When Christiano Ronaldo went to Real Madrid and, with

Giggs and Scholes getting on in years and Rio Ferdinand and Vidic suffering injuries, he went on, in his last season in charge, to win the league again.

For the record, during that time the club won the Premier League in 1993, 1994, 1996, 1997, 1999, 2001, 2002, 2003, 2007, 2008, 2009 and 2011. With this last one, the club, finally, overtook Liverpool with the greatest number of league titles. The FA Cup was added in 1990, 1994, 1996, 1999 and 2004 with the League Cup, in its various incarnations, in 1992, 2006 and 2009. To this can be added the UEFA Champions League in 1999 and 2008 and the FIFA World Cup, in 2008. Along the way, the club collected the UEFA Super Cup in 1992, the Inter Continental Cup in 1999 and the FA Charity Shield (now the Community Shield) in 1990 (shared), 1993, 1994, 1996, 1997, 2003, 2007, 2008,2009, 2011 and 2012. In amassing these, he has done the double twice and the treble once and probable other combinations that might start getting too arcane to mention. I make that 38 trophies in 26 years at the highest level. The club have also done this playing exciting football. Just how difficult this has been is demonstrated in the performances of the team since Fergie left. Even Jose Mourinho is finding it difficult. Nuff said!

Some Reported Quotes

"I'm privileged to have followed Sir Matt because all you have to do is to try and maintain the standards he set so many years ago".

"At the end of this game, the European Cup will be only six feet away from you and you'll not even be able to touch it if we lose. And for many of you that will be the closest you will ever get. Don't you dare come back in here without giving your all". Half time team talk during the 1999 European Cup Final.

"I remember the first time I saw him. He was 13 and just floated over the ground like a cocker spaniel chasing a piece of silver paper in the wind" On Ryan Giggs.

Sir Matt Busby

Sir Matt Busby was Manchester United. He took over in 1946 when Old Trafford was literally a bomb site and he rebuilt the club. He did so with a footballing philosophy that produced a style of play that continues to this day. If "falling with style" was the definition of flying in Toy Story, winning with style has been United's ethos and, largely, they've done that. Matt Busby started a process that culminated in the team achieving his dream of winning the European Cup. Not a boring 1-0 win but a soaring 4-1. Yes, it was 1-1 at full time but United went on to score three goals in extra time to defeat Benfica, the Portuguese Champions and quite some team in their day. In doing so, they become the first English team to win the pre eminent European trophy. Was there ever a more deserved triumph in football? It has also led on, not necessarily in a seamless manner, to them becoming one of the most dominant clubs in world football.

After the Munich air crash of 1958 that almost cost him his own life and did take those of eight of his players, the famous "Busby Babes", among them, the manager had to rebuild the team. This he did, so that 10 years later, he was able to fulfill his dream and win the trophy that many thought that the "Babes" would bring. Bobby Charlton had developed into the exciting player that many expected and with Dennis Law and George Best, they took United to a new level. Sir Matt resigned in January 1969 and moved upstairs to become General Manager, ending 24 glorious years in charge and a legacy that lives on to this day.

Some Quotes

"It was a very simple team talk. All I used to say was: 'Whenever possible, give the ball to George".

"Nobby Stiles, a dirty player? No, he's never hurt anyone. Mind you, he's frightened a few!"

Bill Nicholson

Bill Nicholson devoted his life to Tottenham and, like Bill Shankly and Sir Matt at their respective clubs, it's to him that Spurs owe their position in English football. Like a stick of seaside rock, he had Spurs written right the way through and resigned as manager when he felt that a new generation of players didn't have quite the same allegiance to the club. Born in Scarborough in 1919, he signed for Spurs as a full professional at the age of 18 making his debut in the first team at Blackburn in October 1938. Unfortunately it was in a 3-1 defeat. The following year heralded the out-break of World War II when Bill joined the Durham Light Infantry as a PT instructor.

By 1948, he had established himself in the right half spot and went on to make 314 appearances for the club. Despite being a regular reserve, he only made one appearance for his country being kept out by Billy Wright. Even that included some sort of record when, scoring within 30 seconds in a 5-2 victory against Portugal in 1951, he became the only player to have scored for England with his first touch and never to play at international level again.

With Bill its right half, the late 1940's and early 1950's saw the creation of the famous "push and run" team under Arthur Rowe with the club winning the old Second and First Division titles in consecutive seasons, scoring 163 goals in 84 matches in the process. Rowe retired in 1954 and, in October 1958, Bill Nicholson was appointed as club manager and a new era began.

The club was then sixth from bottom of the division but, on his first outing as manager, hammered Everton at White Hart Lane 10-4. Has there ever been a more auspicious beginning? This was a new club record only surpassed by another under his management, in 1959/60, when they beat Crewe Alexandra in an FA Cup replay, 13-2. Younger read-ers must wonder what is must have been like to see games like that where a goal was scored, on average, every six minutes. You couldn't go home grumbling at that. Know-ing Spurs supporters, I imagine that some of them did, complaining about the goals that were missed.

Within two years, the club was to carve its place in football history by becoming the first team in the 20th Century to win the league and cup double, in 1960/1. In that season, they dominated the league , scoring 115 goals in the process and winning the first eleven games outright. The following season they won the FA Cup again and just missed a European Cup final place being defeated, over two legs, by Benfica after a perfectly good goal from one James P Greaves was disallowed for offside and with Dave Mackay hitting the bar. History was again written when, in May 1963, they beat the favourites, Athletico Madrid, by a resounding 5-1 to become the first English team to win a European trophy, the Cup Winners' Cup. Four years later, they beat Chelsea, to win the first all London FA Cup final, their third FA Cup win in seven years. This was followed by the League Cup in 1971 and 1973 with the UEFA Cup in between in 1972. Glory years indeed.

Judged by what he did and how he behaved, Billy Nick was one of the greats. Look at the players on my list of greats that he brought to the club. Yes I know, I could be wrong on both counts and that two wrongs don't make a right. Most Spurs supporters and any objective observer of the game, would include him in their list of all time great English managers and he's certainly in mine. We wouldn't have had that special Spurs heritage without him.

In September 1974, at the age of 55, Bill Nicholson resigned as manager; a sad day for Spurs supporters, most of whom were shocked by the news. It is said that he felt that the game had changed so that how it had become and his upbringing and ideals were not compatible. However, the man himself said that he was burned out and needed a rest. He left with a dignity that was typical of that upbringing and, possibly, reflected more the manners of the era in which he'd been brought up. If that is so, it is to the detriment of us all. Perhaps reflective of this was the fact that he and his family lived in a modest three bedroom house in Creighton Road, a stones' throw from the ground only moving to the more leafy climes of Hertfordshire in the last years of his life.

In 1991, he was awarded the title of Club President and died on 23 October 2004, another sad day. Since joining as an apprentice in 1936, he had served the club in just about every capacity from boot boy to club president, over a period of 68 years.

Bill Nicholson set the standards for the club and many Spurs' managers have found him a hard act to follow. Indeed, you could argue that the club has been striving to reach his level of success ever since. So, he remains an icon for Spurs supporters and his style of football a yardstick as to how the beautiful game could and should be played. Indeed, one of the tributes paid to him was that "His legacy is to have left forever something that all Spurs teams and staff should aspire to: that is to play football in a correct, honourable and entertaining manner."

There are quite a few quotes from the man although the ones that I've seen, unfortunately, show none of the wit of Shanks or Cloughie. They do, however, show the man's dedication to the game and the club he served for so many years.

One quote attributed to the manager was one that was actually coined by Danny Blanchflower. However, I include it here as it seems a fitting tribute to the man himself. "It is better to fail aiming high than to succeed aiming low. And we of Spurs have set our sights very high, so high, in fact, that even failure will have in it an echo of glory."

"It's been my life, Tottenham Hotspur and I love it".

"When it's played at its best, football remains the greatest game of all and Tottenham, so close to my heart, is still, to me, the greatest club".

"I always said that it was an honour to serve Tottenham Hotspur and I feel the same every time I walk back into the stadium".

Brian Clough

Probably the greatest manager England never had. It is difficult to add much to what has already been said many times over. Idiosyncratic, opinionated, conceited (Old Big Head) and some sort of genius in moulding footballers into teams that could win even the ultimate prizes. Except, famously, the FA Cup. Derby and Nottingham Forest were not noted for their achievements when he took over and have also not been noted for them since he left. Unfashionable clubs that they were, under his, and Peter Taylor's, tutelage, they won League titles and, in Forest's case, two European Cups. Not one, mind you, but two, just to show that the first was no fluke.

Originally from Middlesbrough, he played for the club from 1955 until 1961, scoring 197 goals in 212 matches before moving to neighbouring Sunderland. There he scored 54 goals in 61 matches before a cruciate ligament injury ended his career in December 1962 at the age of 27. He then took up the manager's post at Hartlepool where he invited Peter Taylor to join him and, in 1967, was approached by Derby County. The rest, as they say, is history.

Needing an experienced head for his young side, in 1967, he took Dave Mackay from Spurs to captain the team, then in the old Second Division. They were promoted the following year and went on to take the First Division title in 1972. The following season they lost in the semi final of the old European Cup to Juventus. Amid accusations that officials had been bribed, Clough, in typical fashion, called them "cheating bastards". Unfortunately, he then fell out with the club's board of directors and left in 1973.

His career went a bit skew whiff for a while with spells at Brighton, where he stayed, with Peter Taylor, for a little under a year and, infamously, Leeds United. He and Peter Taylor parted company at Brighton and Cloughie moved to Elland Road on his own. He was to last 44 days, from July until September 1974, falling out with just about all the star players during that time. It was not a meeting of minds and, more importantly, footballing philosophy. He is, famously, reputed to have gathered the players together and told them to throw all their medals away because of the manner in which he considered they'd been won. The players revolted and he was sacked. Given the differences and the animosity that existed between them, both of which were well known at the time, you have to ask yourself whatever made the board think that it could possibly work. At which point, please refer back to the chapter on appointing managers.

He wasn't out of work for long and, in January 1975, took over at Nottingham Forest; then in nearly the same situation as it is today, that is, not particularly successful. Over the next few years, he transformed the club, winning promotion to the First Division within two seasons and the league championship and league cup in their first season in the upper division. Under Clough, the club went on to retain the League Cup and completed that season by winning the European Cup, the smallest city ever to do so. The following season 1980, they won the European Cup again, beating a Hamburg team which included Kevin Keegan in his prime, and reached a third successive League Cup Final; only to be beaten by Wolves by 1 – 0 with a 67th minute goal from Andy Gray. The club would win the League Cup once more in 1989 and again, the following year, the latter with a win over Oldham. The FA Cup would, however, always remain out of his reach as manager with one appearance being the match in which they were beaten by Spurs.

Suffering from the effects of a long term drinking habit he retired, at the end of the 1992/3 season when, after 18 years with the club, it was relegated. However, such esteem was he held in that, it was reported that fans of both Derby County and Nottingham Forest mourned together following his death at the age of 69 of stomach cancer; just one month after that of Bill Nicholson. A memorial service, held at the Derby Ground, a club that he admitted regrets over leaving, was attended by more than 14,000 people.

Cloughie was the master of the quote, many of which typify his attitude to the game and to life in general. Here is just a selection:

Reflecting his failure to get the post of England manager, "I'm sure that the England selectors thought that if they took me on and gave me the job, I'd want to run the show. They were shrewd because that's exactly what I would have done".

Reflecting on his success, "I wouldn't say that I was the best manager in the business, but I was in the top one".

Reflecting on the importance of passing the ball along the ground, "If God had wanted us to play football in the clouds, he'd have put grass up there".

Reflecting on his reputation for getting things done, "Rome wasn't built in a day, but I wasn't on that particular job".

Reflecting on his reputation for being conceited, "On occasions I have been bigheaded. I think most people are when they get into the limelight. I call myself "Old big head" just to remind myself not to be".

On dealing with a player who disagreed with him, "We talk about it for twenty minutes and then we decide that I was right".

After the operation that saved his life, "Don't send me flowers when I'm dead. If you like me, send them while I'm alive".

Reflecting on his drinking, "Walk on water. I know most people out there will be saying that, instead of walking on it, I should have taken more with my drinks. They are absolutely right".

I can still hear his unmistakeable voice saying those things. The world is a more interesting place for him having been born and a less interesting one for his passing.

Bill Shankly

By most accounts, Liverpool was a second rate football team until Bill Shankly took over in December 1959. The late, great "Shanks" took the club and turned it into a force to be reckoned with such that it has won every major honour, except the World Club Championship, and most of these on numerous occasions. A former Scottish International and successful player with, among others, Preston North End, Bill Shankly ended his playing days in March 1949. He took over as manager of Carlisle United but left citing a lack of financial commitment from the directors, a pattern that would repeat itself in his early managerial career until he became manager of Liverpool FC.

The club was then in the bottom half of the old Second Division with poor training facilities and a stadium that was, shall we say, in some need of repair; probably a common enough situation in those days. Shankly did, however, inherit backroom staff that included Bob Paisley and Joe Fagan. From this base, he set about creating a great club with teams that played, as he would say, with a socialist ethic. Players were expected to cover for the mates throughout the game as part of a team just as many supporters did for their neighbours and at work in the factory. In this way, he was perfectly in tune with the supporters and his, and their, working class roots. Ironic that, given that football today probably represents capitalism at its most extreme. Later in life, he would joke that he hadn't had a bath until he was 15 and that poverty gave you a sense of humour. Football, for him and many others, was a way of not having to go down the mines.

Shankly, in what was to be his usual fashion, turned weakness into strength. With the training ground in a terrible state, he is reputed to have organised for the players to meet at Anfield first and then take the bus to Melwood so that they had the chance to get together before training and help create a team spirit. He also introduced a number of other innovations in the players' diets and training methods; keep it simple, pass and move. The players would then all travel back to Anfield for a meal together. Gradually Shanks and his staff turned Liverpool round, winning promotion to the old First Division in 1960/1. The result was seen in the 1963/4 season when the club won the league championship. The rest, as they say, is history. If it wasn't for Bill Shankly, a folk hero if ever there was one, it may well not have been so.

Shankly too was also a great one for quotes of which those I have listed are but a few.

"If you are first you are first. If you are second you are nothing."

"Some people believe football is a matter of life and death, I am very disappointed with that attitude. I can assure you it is much, much more important than that."

"The socialism I believe in is everybody working for the same goal and everybody having a share in the rewards. That's how I see football, that's how I see life".

Commenting on the plaque that says "This is Anfield" "It's there to remind our lads who they're playing for and to remind the opposition who they're playing against".

To a trainee at the club, "The problem with you, son, is that all your brains are in your head".

"In my time at Liverpool we always said we had the best two teams in Merseyside, Liverpool and Liverpool reserves."

"Of course I didn't take my wife to see Rochdale as an anniversary present, it was her birthday. Would I have got married in the football season? Anyway, it was Rochdale reserves."

Alf Ramsey

Sir Alf Ramsey has to be included, being the only English-man ever lead his country to victory in the World Cup. This makes him still the most successful England manager ever supplementing his record with Ipswich, a previously unheralded club. Ramsey obviously inspired his players yet, to an outsider such as myself, he seemed aloof, someone from a previous generation (which he was) in an England that was going through the major changes that were the "Swinging 60's". Yet, despite this army sergeant major's demeanour, he is said to have allowed his players to call him Alf, unusual, even today. Perhaps much of this was related to his working class background and his dislike of the media. Yet, he had sufficient confidence in his own abilities that, after being appointed as manager in 1963, he stated that England would win the World Cup three years later. The statement was not taken seriously at the time.

Following a successful playing career as a right back with Portsmouth, Southampton, where he turned professional, and Spurs, he also captained England. At Tottenham, he featured in the same team as Bill Nicholson, playing over 250 games for the club. He retired in 1955 and became man-ager of Ipswich Town then in the Third Division South. It was there that "The General" developed his strategic vision and tactical awareness to take this small market town club to the First Division title, in their first season in the top flight. In doing so, he found the style that would later make Eng-land World Champions for the first and only time.

Dispensing with wingers, an unheard of concept at the time, he used a 4-3-3 system with overlapping full backs. These "wingless wonders", as the press dubbed them, would confuse the opposition and it worked. Sufficient for England to beat the reigning European Champions, Spain, on their own ground in December 1965, seven months before the World Cup finals. The rest, as they say, is history. In a final where Germany equalised for a second time, right at the death, necessitating extra time, Ramsey urged his players not to sit down at the end of the match or show any signs of weariness that would make the opposition think that they were tired. "You've beaten them once", he said, "Now go out and bloody beat them again. When the final whistle blew, he, famously, can be seen sitting on the bench when all around him were celebrating wildly.

Four years later, in 1970, despite having, probably, a better team that in 1966, and being 2-0 up to Germany in the quarter finals, England lost 3-2. Some thought that it was down to Ramsey's substitutions, other to the fact that Gordon Banks was not in goal. Whatever, he was sacked, ignominiously by the FA in 1974, when the Chairman, Leo McKinstry is reported to have said that "England's most successful manager would have had a legacy fit for a hero had it not been for the malevolence of the FA Chief Executive at the time". Sir Alf Ramsey died in April 1999 in a nursing home where the bills were paid by his successor at Ipswich, Sir Bobby Robson.

Whatever the FA did, however, he remains the only England manager to win the World Cup. Quite an epitaph that.

Bob Paisley

Bob Paisley was probably the least likely looking top football manager. He seemed more slippers and cardigan than tracksuit and football boots. Yet, until Sir Alex, he was probably the most successful manager in the history of English football. Like Bill Nicholson, his association with one club, in this case Liverpool, spanned 50 years as a player, physiotherapist, coach and manager. In the latter capacity, between 1974 and 1983, he managed the club to six league titles, three European Cups, one UEFA Cup, three League Cups, five Charity Shields and a UEFA Super Cup. He is still the only manager in English football to win three European Cups. Not a bad record for someone who looked like your favourite uncle and was, perhaps, not a role model for some of the more "media oriented" managers of today.

Terry Venables

"He is not only the outstanding coach in the country, he is also a clever, shrewd and motivated tactician." Quote from Sir Alf Ramsey in 1994.

I include El Tel as he's been the great "might have" in English football. The only player, at that time, to be capped at every level and the youngest ever captain of Chelsea, he could, in my view, been the greatest Spurs and England manager ever. The football he produced while with these teams, both under achievers, was wonderful to watch. Witness the 4-1 defeat of Holland, no bad team, in the 1996 European Championships. I remember matches with Spurs when the opposition didn't even seem to have the same coaching manual. One, as I've mentioned earlier, with Neil Ruddock receiving the ball on the right wing! Before he was sacked, he led Spurs to that FA Cup win of 1991 following on from the semi final defeat of Arsenal and that Gascoigne wonder goal.

It came near to total football but, as ever with El Tel, it ended in tears as it did with England. I read somewhere that the FA wanted him to be interviewed before he was reappointed and that Alan Sugar had told him to sack someone, a decision with which he disagreed. In both cases, he is supposed to have refused. In the case of the FA, saying that he didn't do auditions. Part of me hopes that this is so because it represents some sort of principle. Probably not a term that would be used by those in the media in regard to much that is professional football at the highest level.

Unfortunately, Terry seems to be the sort of person who needs to be involved in lots of different areas of life at the same time. From inventing the "Thing a Me Wig", a wig that could be worn so that women could go out with their hair in rollers, to singing, writing books and television scripts, inventing board games to owning a night club, football didn't seem to be enough. Yet football coaching and management is what he excelled at.

So El Tel will always be "the great maybe" and we will never know how good that could have been. Shame. He would probably say that a career that, outside football, has included all the activities listed above, wasn't bad. Personally, I would like to have seen what he really could have done as a manager with Spurs. Such is life, especially at Tottenham. It's often what might have been.

Arsene Wenger

I now include "The Professor" which, given his current travails, might seem obtuse, especially for a Spurs' supporter. Yet I do for his overall effect on the game in this country. Had he been a little more pragmatic, he might have been right up the very top, but he isn't either of these. However, he has been a credit to the game and for that and what he has done, I include him.

Virtually unheard of, at least in England when, in 1996, he took over a club with almost the same name, the man has moulded an organisation so that was able to identify bargains and improve them while producing teams that demonstrate the beautiful game as it should be played. Not only that but he took over a football culture that held the line and ground out results. "Boring Arsenal" wasn't just a chant, it reflected what people saw. He changed that. Furthermore, in that amazing season of 2003/4, despite the financial constraints imposed by the new stadium, "The Invincibles" won the Premiership by remaining undefeated all season. The record read 26 wins and 12 draws. Moreover, he did this by playing football as it should be played, albeit a little too over elaborately at times. Along the way, he picked up bargains, turned them into great players, used them for some years, got rid of them for ridiculously high prices and, just when you wondered why, you saw how less well they play for their new clubs. Brilliant! He may have found it hard to replicate that early success because such perfection is difficult to repeat. Anyone can cook egg and chips, it takes someone special to win Michelin stars and Arsene is among the cordon bleu of football managers. He won't stop trying and thank god he doesn't.

Unfortunately, he is now trying in another way and that is the patience of many of the club's supporters; the youngest of whom have little memory of what it was like before he took over. So this man, who appears obsessed with the game, is now in, probably, his last two years with the club. At which point, despite their recent and marvellously unexpected win over Chelsea in the FA Cup, I still feel that, if he was able to change things, he would have done by now. So, whatever you do during that time, Arsene, and I know you will, have a care for your legacy and make sure that you leave with respect and fond memories. After all, even Spurs are ahead of you now and that's something that will be difficult for the club's supporters to accept. Moreover, surely you wouldn't want to be left in the position of one of your arch rivals who was jeered on his return to the club that owes him a great deal. No names, as I'm pretty sure that you wouldn't like to be so compared.

Jose Mourinho

I have a special category for Jose and not just because of his moniker "The Special One". That category is the "almost great" and is included because, with his track record, he simply can't be ignored. However, when even those fans to whom he delivered in abundance, now abuse him in my view, the term great shouldn't be applied.

Unfortunately, despite the fact that those who know him personally talk of his qualities as a person, his demeaning of others only demeans him, in my eyes. His "win at all costs" attitude and the siege mentality that he uses to generate success, seems to spill over into divisiveness and unpleasantness. Witness the shenanigans in his last season at Chelsea where he returned as "the happy one" and was sacked looking like "the angry one"; this after winning the league championship before the team collapsed the following season. The appalling treatment of the club's physiotherapist seemed to sum it all up. So despite his amazing record, he comes with the baggage that I find unpleasant and, for that reason, this incredibly successful manager isn't one of my personal greats. It would be something if he could be and, if he stays at United for the rest of his career and makes them successful while adhering to the style of football that the supporters expect, then he might well be. Still, as someone who is now on his sixth career, I can understand why he might not want to.

Mauricio Pochettino

On this one, I have my fingers crossed and some genuine expectation which, at the time of writing and with a few provisos, might put the current manager in real contention. Those provisos are that he stays around, as Sir Alex did at Manchester United, and that he develops, as he now seems to be doing, beyond the one style pressing game that is his modus operandum. If that continues and he actually delivers that winning, attractive football that all supporters want and which Spurs' ones seem to want more than most, then future generations might well add his name to the list. And wouldn't that be something?

Common Factors

So, is there a common background, a shared cultural heritage that set these managers apart? Well, not so much nowadays, although there did seem to have been in the past. However, most footballers then probably had similar backgrounds so it is to be expected that managers would have had too. So, what were these?

Well, this may be a bit of cod psychology but one that stands out and that is what they often weren't, which was players at the very highest level. The exception might have been Brian Clough had his career not been ended early by injury. So, maybe those managers had some inner drive related to having something still to prove. In addition, a disproportionate number seem to have been Scots, from poor backgrounds, played in the middle of the park and tended not to suffer fools gladly. It always seemed as though their background and that determination to win provided them with the springboard to achieve. Like everything else, though, life was simpler all those years ago while the rose tinted glasses don't get any less tinted as the years go by, not in football anyway. The trouble is, though, that most of them were one offs who left their successors with a hard act to follow when what was needed as a legacy was a system that operated almost irrespective of the personality of the manager. That way sustainability lies.

In that respect, Liverpool are an interesting example using that period from when Bill Shankly took up the reins in 1959 until Kenny Dalgleish left, the first time, in February 1991. For 32 years under these two with Bob Paisley and Joe Fagan in between, the club's "Boot Room" culture operated with each manager following almost seamlessly from the previous one. Starting with winning the old First Division Championship, they won 13 league titles, the FA Cup five times, the European Cup, as it was then, three times , the League Cup four times plus numerous Charity Shields, EUFA Cups, and European Super Cups. Other than the Premiership, they have since won other trophies although, with the demise of the boot room, not anywhere near as many. With only four managers over that whole period, it is an object lesson in how to run a football club successfully and it's surprising that, even today, it seems not to be the norm.

It's not that clubs don't aspire to it, they obviously do. It would make no sense not to. So why doesn't it happen? The answer is "I'm not really sure", although that former England International probably had a point as did Terry Venables. Those and the more international, prestige oriented people with little previous experience or knowledge of the game, who are now involved by virtue of their wealth. It is quite likely that a proportion of these will be keen to exercise their power despite that lack of relevant experience or knowledge. The fact that one or two of these have stretched to the limit the Premier League, Football League and FA's own rules as a "fit and proper person" to own a football club, also adds to the mix.

So, we have the same names cropping whenever a vacancy arises along with foreign managers, one or two of whom appeared not to be too fluent in English at the time that they were appointed. Given that getting your message over and raising and maintaining morale are crucial requirements for the post, just how this was meant to be achieved is unclear. When things don't map out as expected, the manager is sacked. Somehow, those who made the decision to appoint this manager, get off scot free and even get to choose the next one. It beggars belief but it's no fairytale. We see it at work season after season. Many of us, mere fans, are often left scratching our heads while keeping our fingers crossed; no mean feat in itself. We hope against hope and that sustains us, as well as the game itself. Perhaps that, too, is a common factor.

So, I'm not sure that today there is the same common background that there used to be and that's understandable. It may be that there is, instead, a different and more considered one from the new breed of young managers. These include the current Spurs' manager plus Eddie Howe, Sean Dyche, Jurgen Klopp, Paul Clements and Chris Hughton among others. The kings are dead, long live the kings.

Perhaps that sign in Sir Alex Ferguson's office when he was at United, "Ah'm fie Govan", may be the last relic of that old brigade. Although, maybe, clubs are just much more difficult to manage these day and that this new breed is a response to that. What is also interesting is that the most successful, in my list, doesn't include any of the great players. Maybe they couldn't understand that not everyone is as gifted as they were or as hard working. Perhaps the Kevin Keegan Syndrome is real. Finally, I'm getting older, so the common factors these days may just be their youthfulness!

Amazing Games
and Wonder Goals

These are amazing games that I've been to or watched live on television and, based on nothing more than memory. Unfortunately some of them include Spurs losing but in, for what any other team would be, an unbelievable way. So they are selective and even more biased and less factual than anything that has gone before. Perhaps the title of this chapter should really read "Games that have remained in my memory".

Spurs v Man Utd

You could pick any number of these but, as a Spurs fan, I prefer to go back to the old days for my first choice. To a time when Spurs v United or United v Spurs was one of the highlights of the season; a match to look forward to with anticipation that did not usually disappoint, especially when George Best was playing. At least, that's how I remember it. So which do I choose to demonstrate that? Well, for a start, a 5-1 home win at White Hart Lane followed, in the same season, with a defeat by the same score line at Old Trafford.

It was on 16 October 1965 that league champions Manchester United, featuring Best, Law and Charlton (the holy trinity) came to White Hart Lane. The gates were closed at least half an hour before the kick off with 58,051 fans inside, a figure I remember after all these years. I also remember the noise during that hour before kick off which created the atmosphere and set the tone for the spectacle that followed. Apart from the score, what was interesting was that Spurs still featured the last regular players of the double years in Maurice Norman, at centre half, and Dave Mackay, at half back. Happy times indeed.

Spurs took a 2-0 lead into the dressing room at half time with goals from Gilzean and Neil Johnson, a young player who used to run his heart out. Greaves, Clayton and Jimmy Robertson made it 5-0 before Bobby Charlton got a consolation goal for United. Greaves' goal can still be seen on the internet. Reports say that, following moves involving eleven passes, Mackay threaded the ball through to Jimmy who turned and wheeled past two defenders before slotting the ball past the goalie. Watch it if you can, it's a wonderful example of the man at his best.

Nine weeks later, Spurs travelled to Old Trafford for the return match. They, in their turn, were trounced by the same score line in front of a crowd of 39,511 with Cliff Jones scoring the only Spurs goal. Fast forward nearly 47 years to Saturday 29 September 2012, a date that will remain long in the memory of all Spurs fans. Winning at Old Trafford for the first time in 23 years. 2 - 0 up in just over half an hour and playing United off the pitch for the whole of the first half. They were hanging on at the end but, hang on they did. It was, probably, Andre Vilas Boas' best match as manager. I left the pub hoarse and, probably, a foot off the ground.

Spurs v Burnley

It was the 4th round of the FA Cup at White Hart Lane against rivals, Burnley, then a big club, in front of 50,611 fans, myself among them. Spurs were 0-2 down within 20 minutes with goals by Willie Irvine, the opposing centre forward. It seemed that they were out of the match until Alan Gilzean took over. Two from Gilly meant that the scores were level at half time with Spurs looking as though they would win. Unfortunately Irvine scored his third goal and the atmosphere changed. Cometh the moment, cometh the man and Gilzean netted a third. If I remember it was a low drive from outside the penalty area. Fortunately for the home side, with minutes remaining, Frank Saul, dear old Frank Saul, scored the winner and me, and thousands of other Spurs fans, went home delirious.

Chelsea v Spurs Carling Cup Final

After many years of defeats and after being a goal down, Spurs finally beat Chelsea to win the Carling Cup after being 1-1 at fulltime. Not so much great or memorable match but included because of the sheer lift it gave all Spurs fans on the day and one that gave hope again for the future. Unfortunately, in true Spurs fashion, only for those hopes to be dashed in the following season with two points from the first eight games. Still, it was great while it lasted.

Spurs v Man City 3-4

Not great for any Spurs' supporter, this match, with any other club, would have been filed under unbelievable. Yet, for those home fans who watched it, they knew that it wasn't. Unbelievable, no, inevitable, yes. In fact, given the nature and history of both clubs, it could have gone either way until half time. Rather like pushing a heavy roller up hill, once it got to the top, there was that split second when it could have either rolled back the way it had come or carried on gathering momentum. In either case, it was taking you, the spectators, with it. There was no stopping its relentless course. Unfortunately, it was Spurs who were left surveying the wreckage when the match ended.

It was February 2004 and an evening match that had started so promisingly for Spurs when Ledley King scored after only two minutes and with the team 3-0 up at half time. With Nicolas Anelka substituted after less than half an hour, City's best hope of scoring was withdrawn to be replaced by John Macken who, would you believe it, delivered the decisive blow in the 90th minute? Yet when Joey Barton, who else, was shown a red card at the end of the first half, it seemed all over. If you're not Tottenham, that is. Goals from Distin, Bosvelt and Shaun Wright-Phillips brought the tie to level pegging by which time all Spurs supporters knew what would happen next. Ten minutes later, with the referee about to blow the whistle, Macken headed beyond Kasey Keller for the winner. City went on to the local derby that awaited them in the next round. Spurs fans went home knowing, as only a Spurs fan could at that time, that, against 10 men and with the team 3-0 up, once the opposition scored, the result was inevitable.

Spurs v Aston Villa 5-5

Another to be filed under unbelievable but inevitable. Laurie Brown, ex Arsenal, was at centre half and, for those with long memories, that may say it all. 5-1 up by half time and yet Alan

Mullery had to clear off the line towards the end of the match to prevent Villa winning 5-6. Tony Hateley, the Villa centre forward scored four goals in the second half, probably all with his head. He also played for Chelsea and, I think, Liverpool. Not so hot with his feet, he even used to go for knee level crosses with his head and, it is thought by some, to have even scored a penalty in the same way. Laurie Brown was not too hot before this match. I suspect this was his nadir as, later that season, he was transferred. Perhaps his mistake had been to open the scoring on that day, a feat which might have turned his head even before Tony Hateley did.

Southampton v Spurs

It was on the 1st of March 1995 in an FA Cup 5th round replay. I watched it opposite our local pub where Malcolm, a mate, had a photographic studio in Pratt Street. It was the night that Ronny Rosenthal, formerly of Liverpool (Rocket Ronnie) became, for a short while, a cult figure. 2-0 down at half time. Two goals from Ronnie, known, if I remember, more for those he missed than those he scored, put Spurs on level terms just before the hour mark. He then scored a third goal which was followed by goals from Sheringham, Anderton and Nick Barmby to give Spurs a 2-6 win. What I remember is us all laughing at the sheer unbelievability of it especially when Grobelaar went one way to get the ball only for it to swerve (or did it hit someone on the way) while he tried vainly to change direction in mid air. It may have been the drink, but it was amazing.

Arsenal v Spurs

The venue, Wembley Stadium, The date, April 1991. Was it really that long ago? The teams, Arsenal and Spurs and the match, the FA Cup semi final and just this one to win to get to the final, which, if they won it, would then be for a record number of times. They did with Gascoigne's glorious 35 yard free kick and two goals from Lineker. I watched it in a fellow supporter's house and a crowd of mates in Richmond. It was one of those days when all went right with the world. To beat the old enemy and with such an unbelievable free kick was superb. Life should be like that all the time.

Arsenal v Spurs (again)

Just to demonstrate that good things (a bit like miracles) didn't only happen hundreds of years ago, here was a beauty in which Spurs came out on top without actually winning. It was October 2008 and Senor Ramos had been sacked leaving the club with two points from eight games and relegation staring it in the face. Three days after being appointed and Harry had to take Spurs to the Emirates. The omens, despite the ability of new managers to lift teams, were not good. Little did any of us know the drama that was about to unfold and which team would be left celebrating as the match reached its climax in stoppage time.

David Bentley, against one of his former clubs, scored the sort of goal that you see once in a season. A forty yard volley past Almunia and Spurs were 0-1 up within 13 minutes. Unfortunately, Arsenal then took control of the game with goals from Sylvestre, Gallas, within seconds of the start of the second half, and Adebayor to put them 3-1 up. In what now appears to be a pattern with Arsenal, they then wasted chances with their need to show just what wonderful football they could play. Some might call it over elaboration.

In the 67th minute Darren Bent pulled one back for Spurs only for Robin van Persie to put Arsenal in the driving seat again within a minute, scoring his 50th goal for the club. Game over, we thought. Yet with two minutes remaining Jenas scored from the edge of the area to make it 4-3. Still game over, we thought. Four minutes of injury time were shown and, in the last of these, Luca Modric hit the post. Fortunately for Spurs, Aaron Lennon was on hand to put the ball into the net from close range. Game now really over and Spurs had drawn at the Emirates to start the process of staving off relegation. Having taken just two points from their first eight games, they were now in a sequence that would take ten points from a possible twelve including matches against Liverpool and Bolton, traditionally teams that had beaten them in recent years. The belief was back and, despite further setbacks, Spurs would go on to finish in a creditable eighth position.

Inter Milan v Spurs

It was 20th October 2010 and the Champion's League match that announced Gareth Bale to the world. Spurs were drawn against Inter Milan with the first leg away. Inter were a formidable team managed by one Rafael Benitez and had, in Maicon, the best left back in the world at the time. They were 1 - 0 down within a minute and 2 - 2 down within 7 minutes with the latter a penalty for which Gomez was given a red card. By half time, the score was 4 - 0 and it could have been six. Enter stage left one Gareth Bale. Running, with the ball from his own half, he left his opponent for dead, 4 - 1. That remained the score until the final few minutes when that man scored two more; each one powered in with that left foot. It was a one man display of speed, power and intent that you just don't see very often. Gareth Bale was simply unstoppable that night and we, Spurs' supporters were on cloud 9 and beyond.

Spurs went on to win the return match, two weeks later, 3-1, with Gareth, once again, destroying the opposition. It was probably then that the crowd began calling, "Taxi for Mr Maicon". I have it all on a memory stick somewhere, courtesy of my son, Matt.

Wonder Goals

Individual goals stick in the memory at least as much as great matches and, probably, more so. Not for any other reason than that it's easier to remember a single event than a whole game. At White Hart Lane and at other grounds where Spurs have played, probably too many to mention. However, here are my memories with the first being a little bit of a cheat although, given the quality of the goal, the fact that it was scored by a former Spurs' player and regarded by a former manager as the greatest ever, gives me, I hope, somewhat of a license. Added to which was the fact that it was scored against our north London rivals which adds a certain piquancy.

It was the 1995 UEFA Cup Winners' Cup Final between Real Zaragoza and Arsenal with 20 seconds of extra time left and the score at 1-1. Fifty yards out, Nayim, who had been a favourite when he played for Spurs, seeing that Seaman was off his line and that two of his own team mates were offside, took the ball on his chest and, knowing exactly what he was doing, hit the ball to send it high but dipping, with accuracy and pace, beyond the goalie's despairing reach such that he and the ball dropped into the back of the net. Arsenal had lost.

In the studio, Terry Venables, then an ITV commentator, was asked where he placed the goal in his all time list. "In the top" slight pause for breath, "one" he replied. I walked to our local after the match to find many of the bar staff in their Arsenal colours. "Don't say a word" I was told. I didn't need to, the extremely large grin on my face said it all.

For the club itself though, there are so many to choose from. How could it not be so from a club that has featured Greaves, Gilzean, Jones, Chivers, Ginola, Hoddle, Ricky Villa, Ossie, Chris Waddle, Jurgen Klinsmann, Teddy Sheringham, Gascoigne, Berbatov and now Harry Kane. Where do you start? Well, by acknowledging that, although skill is prerequisite, memory and the occasion also play a large part, so here goes.

Well you could Google "Berbatov's goals for Spurs" and watch 8½ minutes of pure joy. 46 of them, scored with right foot, left foot and head. Apart from the five tap ins and four penalties, the remaining 37 were wonderful examples of goal scoring at the highest level. So, I have to choose one of his and can do nothing else except select the one against Charlton, his 22nd of the season, 2006/7. Goalie to Ledley King, a long pass to Dimitar just inside the opposition half on the left wing. A delightful flick of the foot took the ball past the defender with Dimitar in close pursuit and control. At which point, there was only one conclusion and it was one delivered with Berabtov's usual aplomb. 40 metres of ground was covered with the defender doing his legitimate best to prevent the inevitable. The ball was duly dispatched and the goal keeper beaten from distance. Game over.

As for the others, I've decided to opt for one by David Ginola; this one against Barnsley in the FA Cup in March 1999. My god, that's nearly 20 years ago. David picked up the ball on the left touchline, 35 metres from goal, and skipped past the first defender. He then waltzed through two more before tucking a low side-foot past the goalkeeper with his right foot. That season, he was rightly voted PFA and Football Writers' Player of the Year.

Two more, each defined by the quality and wonder of the goal as well as by the occasion. Ricky Villa in the FA Cup Final replay against Manchester City in 1981 and Paul Gascoigne's unbelievable free kick from 35 yards (32 metres in new money) against Arsenal in the FA Cup semi final at Wembley in 1991.

Against City, the first match had finished 1-1, the 100th Final, and Ricky had been substituted after a not very happy afternoon. The replay, five days later and also at Wembley, however, was a very different affair. Ricky scored in the eighth minute to put Spurs ahead but with 14 minutes left to play, the score was 2-2. With the game entering the closing stages, Ricky, 30 yards from goal and slightly to the left, received the ball and set off for the goal. Twisting one way and then the other, he left Tony Caton, Ray Ranson and then Tony Caton, again, in his wake before slotting the ball past their goalie, Joe Corrigan. 3-2 and the Cup belonged to Tottenham again. Ricky's goal is still spoken of as the best cup final goal ever.

Paul Gascoigne's goal also will never be forgotten especially as it was against the Gooners and saw Spurs on their way to another FA Cup Final. Watch it on You Tube. Against an Arsenal team that had only lost once in the league that season and with Gascoigne only recently returned from a hernia operation, they were probably not favourites. That was turned on its head with Gazza at his imperious best.

After only five minutes Spurs were awarded a free kick in a position 35 yards from the Arsenal goal and almost centrally on the pitch. Gascoigne took a simple run up. "He's not going to have a go from there. He is, you know" commented Barry Davies followed by "That is Schoolboys' Own stuff" as the ball tucked itself away just inside the top left hand corner of the goal and beyond David Seaman's reach. It showed Gazza at his mischievous and majestic best. To score it he used three attributes, his awesome power with a shot, his expertise in placing a ball with such precision from distance and the sheer audacity to do it.

I don't think anyone in an Arsenal shirt, at least on the pitch, moved until the goalkeeper picked the ball out of the back of the net by which time Paul Gascoigne was off and running towards the centre circle. A second goal from Gary Lineker followed by one from Arsenal seemed to set the match up. It was not to be for the Gooners and Spurs were in the final, a match in which they were to beat Brian Clough's Nottingham Forest. I believe to this day that it was Gascoigne's performance for the hour that he was on the pitch, and that goal, that knocked the stuffing out of Arsenal and won the match for Spurs.

Also, for examples of sheer mischievous consistency and no little skill and effort, try to get a look at any by one Jimmy Greaves. You won't be disappointed.

Other Memories

Sometime in the late 1970's my children were in Harrogate and I was in London. They came to see me and I went to meet them at Kings Cross Station. I got there early and stood at the end of the platform waiting for the train to come in. As I waited I could hear singing from the far end of the station and realised that it was from another train arriving. As it drew nearer, the singing got louder until the train drew to a halt and the doors opened at which point, passengers got off and started to fill the platform. I can't remember which particular Scot's song it was but it heralded the arrival of supporters coming to watch their team play England at Wembley. It was an emotional and uplifting noise. The gathering of the clans, if you like. Waiting for the train from Yorkshire, I watched in amazement as one fan, and I am clear in my mind on this, walked down the platform with a crate of McEwans in his arms. Had no one told him that you could buy McEwans in London and whether he would be able to take it all the way to Wembley would be a matter of some conjecture? As I write this, I don't believe that it happened but I'm sure that it did.

In the 1960's, Spurs often used to play Glasgow Rangers

in pre season friendlies and, as usual, I settled in my patch in the corner of the ground. After a while I found myself surrounded by Rangers' supporters and the banter flowed. Friendly but often caustic. One Scot was none too sober and had his hand on one pole of a banner. Lucky really as it was the only thing that prevented him from falling over. I mentioned to one of his mates that they needed to keep an eye on "their mate". "He's no mate of ours" was the reply, "He's a Motherwell supporter who we happened to meet at Glasgow Station. He probably doesn't even realise that he's in London". I took it as part of the humour but I was never sure whether or not it was meant as a joke. Certainly they were more interested in the match than his welfare so how, or even whether, he got home is anyone's guess.

My son, Matt, must have been about eight and we lived in Stevenage. The United match came along and so we went. On the way home, we got to Seven Sister's Station to get the tube to King's Cross. The area was packed and the London Underground staff were regulating the crowd by keeping the gates shut and letting people down to the platforms when a train had cleared enough passengers there. As they opened the gates to let us in, no matter how hard I tried to hold onto him, Matt got dragged away from me into the crush.

I panicked although I needn't have. A large United supporter reached over, grabbed Matt by the scruff of the neck and put him on his shoulders. "Don't worry, mate. See you at the bottom of the escalator". Telling Matt also not to worry, off he set with me some yards behind, still hemmed in. Above the heads of the crowd, I kept my eyes firmly on my son, waving to let him know that it was OK. Eventually, I got to the foot of the escalator where the United supporter waited to hand over a worried son to a grateful father. In response to my expressions of gratitude, a northern accent said something like "No problem. Take care of him, mate. See you at Old Trafford for the return", before he disappeared into the crowd.

The point is that, outside had been mayhem, yet this supporter showed that whatever side you were on, you had more in common than you didn't have. If he ever reads, this, thanks. The boy you rescued is now an adult with a son of his own.

Another little story that demonstrates humanity and football supporters in a good light before I finish this chapter. A little over 13 years ago, after a short illness, my wife's father died. In organising the funeral service, she and other members of the family wanted a poem they'd heard. It contained the phrase, "I'm not gone, I'm just in the other room" or something like that. Gaynor, my wife, couldn't find it and I mentioned it to Matt. "Don't worry, Dad, I'll find it for you" was his response. I didn't know it at the time but he went on to one of the Spurs' message boards and e mailed the responses to me. Not only had they found the poem; probably not too difficult a task, but they had left messages; complete strangers. One I remember said, "Take care, Matt, sorry to hear of your sad news and hope all is as well as it can be". Many thanks to that person for reinforcing my faith in human nature at a time that we were all feeling pretty bloody awful.

The Dark Side of the Game

Now for that part of the book which highlights the dark side of the game and what a dark side it is. In fact, if half of what is described in "Broken Dreams" is true, then many board-rooms should be fumigated at the end of each meeting.

Tom Bower is a respected author, investigative journalist and television producer. He has written exposes of Robert Maxwell, Mohammed Fayed, Richard Branson, Geoffrey Robinson and Conrad Black and in 2003, his book about professional football, was published. Every football supporter should read it. Its sub title, "Vanity, Greed and the Souring of Football" adequately sets the tone for the lies and corruption that he exposes. For any football follower, it doesn't make for a comfortable read. It makes an even less comfortable read for someone, like me, who likes to think that he has put some sort of ethics before profit, in spending much of his working life in the voluntary sector. And who, furthermore, rails against all that which has been exposed over the past few years as corruption and sleaze in politics, the press and the banking world. Yet, can I bring myself to even show some anger about what is portrayed in the book? Would you believe it? I can't.

The reason for this state of affairs, these massive internal contradictions is that I separate the activities on the pitch from those off it. What is more, I don't even try to rationalise that situation. Vain, egotistical, greedy men, often ill mannered and uncouth have a hand in running our national game. Without mentioning any names, you will know who some of them are and, furthermore, you won't be surprised at their individual attitudes and behaviour. Although you may be surprised to read it all so clearly spelt out in plain English, complete with expletives. It does not paint a pleasant picture of the way in which these people behave, among whom are those who made their particular views on the similar uncouth behaviour of a few fans, very plain. It also doesn't paint a particularly uplifting picture of their business ethics. Why doesn't that surprise me? I can only suggest that you read a real eye opener of a book.

It is now 14 years since its publication and I have no way of knowing how much has changed during that time; very little for the better, I suspect. Among other things, it shows that many in the game live in a bubble, apart from the world that the rest of us inhabit. Unfortunately, it is the fans, with their commitment, who sustain this bubble.

Like I said, read the book from which I will merely quote the front cover which says that "To own a Premier League club is the dream of countless businessmen. Each season, millions of passionate football fans follow their team's progress, praying for a championship victory. But, off the pitch, there is a very different agenda where money is the prize; where dubious accounting, billion dollar television deals and puzzling player transfers make men rich. Meticulously researched, "Broken Dreams" is a superbly incisive account of how self interested individuals exploit the sport of football to earn billions of pounds and huge glory." Depressing reading for any fan.

One dark side that is, somewhat, less so these days, is alcohol; something that is a normal part of most peoples' lives along with a degree of overindulgence. In the past it was synonymous with the game and, during the close season, it may still be today to some degree. However, at the elite level, probably much less so than previously, given clubs require the utmost fitness from their players. Yes, there will be transgressions but certainly not at the level of even the recent past. Furthermore, even if players were so inclined, the predominance of smart phones with high quality video capability means that it wouldn't take long, for anyone interested in making a nice little earner, from contacting one of the tabloids with photos or live footage. That's not to say that players don't misbehave; indeed, there's a chapter devoted to it in "The Secret Footballer" largely related to young men with more than enough money having a good time on trips away. Now there's a surprise!

Indeed, those of you who have read the book will be aware of the bubble that he and his peers live in. Indeed, if the depression experienced and feelings expressed are prevalent among Premiership footballers today, one can only feel sorry for them. Not something I ever thought I'd say.

Yet the past, as is often said, is a different country and, certainly, there appear to have been some very successful players with real problems with alcohol; and not so very long ago. Read the biographies and autobiographies if you need evidence. Paul MacGrath, Jimmy Greaves, George Best, Jim Baxter, Tony Adams, Paul Merson, Paul Gascoigne, Malcolm MacDonald and Stan Bowles, to name but a few of the more well known ones. The success of the first of these is especially uplifting given the cards that life dealt him. So, whether it was booze, gambling or women or, in George Best's case, all three, they tended to indulge which make their achievements all the more remarkable.

The wonder is that many more don't succumb; at least to the same degree, given the life that they lead. For a start, the players, like other young people today, live in a world in which drink, other drugs and sex are commonplace. Yet overindulgence, at least in the first two of these, are likely to have a detrimental effect on their careers while their incomes will allow them to partake of all of them without the financial constraints that apply to others. On the other side of the coin, the lives of such players revolve around training for and playing football, hard. Once the match is over, the exultation at winning or the depression of losing also may be difficult to handle. A long return journey with the rest of the team is followed by what? If you are married or settled down, your family are there. If you are single you may wish to do what most single men do, go out with your mates. In most cases that would mean going for a drink where you are likely to stand out as the celebrity or groups of celebrities. You get the picture?

So, life for the top professional footballer today seems to be one in which the rewards are great as are the demands and the temptations. The wonder is that, given their youth, those temptations and their wealth, more of them don't stray from the straight and narrow. The alternative, of course, is that the clubs have first class PR departments. Which brings me on to the matter of gay footballers.

Like the rest of the population, a footballer's sexuality is no one's concern but their own. So the fact that there aren't any openly gay professional footballers in this country is not a surprise. Indeed, in the macho world that is the game, it would be difficult for any of them to come out. To my knowledge, the only one who did, Justin Fashanu, committed suicide. A sad ending for anyone compounded, in his case, by the waste of a talented footballer's life. Where were the clubs he played for and the support he needed or was it offered and rejected? Given the game's history in the way it handles those who don't make it, I suspect that what he needed wasn't available. So, as in other parts of the entertainment industry, why can't those who are gay in the sport come out? I know it's no one's concern but the fact that it is unacknowledged is. After all there are now gay amateur football teams. Still, I don't expect it to happen in the game in England in the immediate future. Shame really, it would provide great role models for young people coming to terms with their sexuality and others still experiencing discrimination. I know all the arguments about changing rooms, team morale and whatever else is trotted out, however, according to the secret footballer it is more to do with the players fearing the fans' attitude. Something I understand but don't buy.

In a team game that is the world of professional football, grown men are known to one another as "Lamps", "JT",

Scholesy and Giggsy. It is part and parcel of a collective effort, creating an atmosphere of camaraderie and inclusion, manifest in use of such nicknames. It was so in the army where I spent 12 years of my life. Unfortunately, just that atmosphere can, by its nature, create a sense of exclusion for those who don't conform to the mores of the group. Individuals who exhibit some "otherness", as was evidenced in Robbie Fowler's very public behaviour toward Graham Le Saux. It appears that Le Saux just happened to read The Guardian. I also know how crass was the attitude of some supporters towards Sol Campbell. It needs to change as, indeed, in the world outside the game, it is doing, fast.

Yet, if government estimates are anywhere near accurate, people who are gay, both male and female, constitute 6% of the population or 3.6 million people. The Premier League is made up of 20 clubs with squads of 25 being registered for each club in addition to an unlimited number of under 21 year olds. That means that there are, at least, 500 registered Premiership players, of which 30 could be gay. I reiterate that it is nobody else's concern what other people do consensually in their sex lives. However, when people are scared to come out, for whatever reason, it would help if someone did and it will happen one day. As, indeed, it now has in two very macho sports.

Former Welsh rugby captain player Gareth Thomas, now retired, came out in 2009. Mind you Gareth is six foot three, weighs 16 stone and won 100 international caps. He tells of coming out with his club captain explaining to him that all his team mates already knew. Thomas' response was "Halle fucking lujah". Interestingly he then says that, individually, his team mates have told him that they have so much time for what he has done. Also, now, openly gay is Puerto Rican boxer Orlando Cruz. At the time, Cruz was rated 4th in the world as featherweight by the WBO.

I somehow can't see anyone in the dressing room or among the fans having the courage to disparage these two, at least to their faces. I'm not saying the fears expressed by the secret footballer aren't real, they obviously are; in the players' heads. So, perhaps, these fears need to be faced up to. We have a "Kick out Racism" agenda, why not a "Respect

164

Gay People" one? Who was it who said that the only thing we have to fear is fear itself? Still, I look forward to the first professional footballer coming out just to help change people's perceptions, which is what this particular rant is all about.

Do I expect any to come out in the not too distant future? Well, yes, I think I do. What I would say to anyone in that bubble who is thinking of doing it is that the following morning the world will still be revolving, as it has done for billions of years, and that that evening the sun will set and the moon appear. In fact, the world will continue much as before and the newspapers that print the news will be recycled by the end of the week. Even homophobic fans will lose interest after a while and you will still be the same quality player that you always were. Lastly, do you think that your team mates don't already know? Gareth Thomas' did. Mind you, it's probably not your team mates that are the real concern especially at certain grounds that could be mentioned.

Lastly racism. Well, the situation is certainly considerably better than it was 30 years ago when black players were fairly regularly abused from the terraces. We hear little of that these days, thank god. Certain individuals notwithstanding, it does seem to be disappearing along with all the other idiotic views that humans have held over the years. The irony of it all is that when we came out of Africa those 70,000 years or so ago, guess what colour we were? Or did only the white ones leave?

So let's remain on our guard while commending the progress that has been made. Is there still racism in football? Yes, there obviously is, much as there is discrimination in all walks of life. It is not, however, confined to the terraces as recent events have shown. So I, for one, will give football supporters a little pat on the back in this area and hope that my words don't come back to haunt me.

One other area where they won't and one that brings out a real anger in me is the sexual abuse of children and young people, information on which, in regard to football, hit the headlines only a few years ago. Now it may not be easy for people to accept this but for someone to do something like that, there has to be a reason and therein lies part of the solution. In the meantime and above all else, there needs to be prevention of the crime and the protection of those children and young people.

Put simply, paedophilia is a heinous activity which, when I was younger, was usually portrayed as the work of strangers and individual "weirdo's". Unfortunately, both of these descriptions painted a false picture. The reality, as we now know (or can admit to) is that much child abuse takes place within families and that many paedophiles operate by getting into just the type of work that gives them access to their targets in the first place. Football, it now seems, isn't immune to this and why should it be? The result has been, as you might expect, devastated lives. Unfortunately, there also seems to have been the lack of the sort of basic procedures in place that are a normal part of the voluntary sector where I've spent much of my working life. Now that it has come to light, there is a degree of dirt being swept under carpets where what is needed is understanding, policies and action. Wouldn't it be good if football could be at the forefront of this movement? Don't hold your breath unless, of course, you're able to do so for some considerable time.

Finally, no book on football is complete without mention of hooliganism. That and football seemed, at one time, to be synonymous with one another. Named in myth, after an Irish immigrant family, a distant relative of the Daligans, no doubt, hooligans attach themselves to football every so often. It isn't endemic in the game or a necessary part of it, despite the views of the tabloid press who like an easy headline most of the time. When I was a child, it was teddy boys, then mods and rockers, most of them now respectable parents and grandparents themselves. Today it is hoodies, chavs and immigrants. No doubt they too will be parents and grandparents in their own good time. Not that many of these are, or were, hooligans in their time but, hey, let's not allow that to get in the way of selling newspapers.

Until, many years later, when some of those newspapers were found out to have been telling less than the truth and claimed that they were only printing what they were told, saying that they had been lied to. Not that they'd ever had problems in not quite telling the truth in the past without too much prompting. No, I know, you couldn't make it up. Which is exactly what they did. After all, football and scapegoats sells papers. Except for The Sun in Liverpool where people still won't buy it.

What is wrong with this attitude is that it fits people into categories which it then proceeds to denigrate. The world and the people who inhabit it are a lot more complex than that, as is obvious to those who care to look. Perceptions are important and we don't need to be fostering any more ill feeling in the world than that which already exists. This attitude is manifest in an old saying that rugby is a game for hooligans played by gentlemen whereas football is a game for gentlemen played by hooligans. It didn't mention those who watch these sports although I think the implication was clear. So when football and hooliganism are being spoken of in the same sentence, please look beyond the easy headlines and deal with the real causes of real problems. That way, you might go some way towards solving them.

Football is tribal so the ingredients for violence are, unfortunately, always there. However, in my personal experience, I have witnessed only one stand up fight, one running fight and some skirmishing, probably three or four times during the years that I used to go to White Hart Lane and a few away grounds. The fight was over as quickly as it had begun and the skirmishes were stamped out by the police also fairly quickly. Interestingly the one real fist fight was between four people all of whom wore smart suits and ties, not exactly the popular image of the football hooligan.

Don't get me wrong, I wouldn't have wanted to have been on the receiving end. My point is I could probably just as easily been on that receiving end anywhere as at a football match or the adjoining streets. So, perhaps, a sense of perspective is needed. Unfortunately, the popular press is not that good at that. To misquote that line in "The Man Who Shot Liberty Valance" when the lie becomes reality, then print the lie. Hell, why wait for it to become reality, just print it anyway.

So, to set it in perspective, hooliganism has been around since time immemorial and, unfortunately, will probably continue. It is something that I have to admit is beyond my comprehension yet it happens. Some people do seem to like fighting and, having spent 12 years in the army, I met one or two of them. This long history includes the Manchester scuttlers of the late 19th century, the razor gangs of the 1950's or the football hooligans of the 1970's. It is also not confined to one strata of society with bullying (surely a form of hooliganism) being pretty rife in public schools I understand, over the years. Did someone mention the Bullingdon Club?

That being said, it's not a problem that can be ignored and even my liberal attitude needs to acknowledge the fact that hooliganism isn't just either casual or organised, small scale and domestic. It may be less prevalent than it used to be at home but, with the advent of the internet and the mobile phone, it can be highly organised and international. This also appears to have its foundation in a macho nationalism that is almost condoned by the governments of those countries concerned. Being international it requires international effort to tackle; just at the time that our own country is turning its back on Europe. What's that old saying that "Those the gods wish to destroy, they first make mad"?

Linked to the wariness of other cultures that seems to exist in our society and the ability of far right groups to use anything within their means to recruit to their cause, vigilance is always necessary. Not only necessary but essential in order that violence can be prevented. Will we ever eradicate it? Well inside sports grounds with seating only (is it possible to have a fight sitting down?), yes, we seem to have, for now. Outside? Well it's quiet these days but you never can tell. Maybe, fight and flight is the male human's default mechanism after all. Others terms with similar initial letters (f and f) would seem to me to be a far nicer way of spending your time. Dark side described, so let's get back to the fun.

The 'Redknapp Years'

The season 2008/9 was just two months old when, after a little over a year in charge, Juande Ramos was sacked. From the heights of winning the Carling Cup Final the previous season, beating both Arsenal and Chelsea in the process, Spurs had amassed only two points from the first eight games and experienced their worst start ever. Even at this early stage, many of us felt that relegation was a real possibility. Thus, the decision, when it came, was not unexpected.

Harry Redknapp was appointed as manager the following day turning the next four seasons into the 'Redknapp Years' and what rollercoaster years they were. From such an inauspicious start, the journey took the club to fourth place in the Premiership, Champions League football and repeats of those glorious European evening matches of years ago. Along the way, the football was a joy to watch. Until, in true Tottenham fashion, Harry too was sacked. After four seasons of football that truly reflected "Audere est facere" we had "Audere est sackere". Has anyone before, after completely turning around a club's fortunes so greatly while remaining true to its traditions, ever been sacked, let alone with just a year left on his contract? Something beyond football was surely at work here. Mind you, Harry didn't do himself any favours with players being quoted as saying that tactics didn't form a great part of their training. His deeply held belief that players should be allowed to express themselves on the pitch does him credit. That doesn't mean though that they shouldn't be just as fit and tactically aware as the teams that they are in competition with. This, something that many Spurs fans felt was the reality of the situation, reflected in the fact that the team had a habit of running out of steam towards the end of a match and losing its way three quarters of the way through the season.

This may have been compounded by the trial over his tax affairs, his handling of the media over the England post and his comments on the need for a new contract when, it was reported that, one wasn't on offer. However, it was also part of a pattern on the pitch from previous years. In addition, there was certainly a feeling that Harry stayed within his comfort zone, both in terms of tactics and the players he brought in. If that is so, it will certainly have had an effect on those players who would, likely, have stayed within their comfort zone too and when a number start to do this, it affects the team's performance. It almost goes without saying that this comfort zone is not accepted in the really successful teams.

Evidence for this can be seen in a quote from a Manchester United player to Dimitar Berbatov after he was transferred from Spurs. It seems he was being taken to task over a lack of effort on one particular occasion. His response, that it was the way he played, was met evidently with the sharp rejoinder, "not in this fucking team, you don't". After three years, Berbatov left United and Martin Jol, his manager at Spurs and then in a similar position with Fulham, was quoted as saying that he had never seen him move about so much in a match. On the other side of the coin, the expectations that Harry and the rest of his management team had raised so highly only made matters worse. Then again, maybe he really had taken the club as far as he could. Being a Spurs' supporter, however, you could see what was coming. What we, the fans, didn't know was that Harry's departure would herald the arrival of Andre Villas-Boas; something that I couldn't understand. Never mind, a little less than 18 months later and he, too, was gone.

At which point, let's get back to the Redknapp Years, where the renaissance started immediately; one in the eye for those pundits who say, as they invariably do when a club is in difficulties, "What difference would a change in manager make?" Well, they were soon to find out when Spurs drew one and won three of the next four games. The draw, an amazing 4-4 away to the arch enemy, Arsenal, in which Spurs were losing by two goals with a minute of normal time to play. The team was transformed and went on to a creditable 8th place in the Premiership and reached the final of the Carling Cup.

The following season was to be an even better one culminating in an away win against Manchester City on the penultimate match of the season. The teams were in contention to see which one would bring European football back to their respective clubs after many barren years. With just 8 minutes left, Peter Crouch headed the goal that meant that it was to be Tottenham. OK, so they lost away to Burnley on the final day after being 2-0 up, but, by that time, it no longer mattered. Threatened by relegation a mere 19 months previously, Harry had brought the glory days back to the club in some style. Yes, there were some low points notably losing, at home, to Hull, Wolves and Stoke; a harbinger of what was to happen in successive seasons. The highs, though, far outweighed them as did that incredible 9-1 thrashing of Wigan. The Wigan goalie was reputed to have been asked what the time was and, before he could answer, the chant came back from the fans, "nearly 10 to 1".

The City match demonstrates one of professional football's better points. It may be divisive in many ways but it does have an ability to unite across the generations and there is too little of that these days. I had seen Mike and Dave in the pub on occasions during the season notably watching the home match against Arsenal when their friend, a Gooner, finished up in tears. We hugged in celebration of beating the old enemy and went our separate ways, on cloud nine. We met again to watch the City match at the end of which three, near strangers, from very different ends of the age spectrum, finished up hugging one another. They were amazed that the person they were hugging had waited 40 years (more than their combined lifetimes) to see Spurs' back in Europe.

After a goalless draw at home to Manchester City on the opening day of the following season, Spurs were initiated into the Champions League with an away match against the Young Boys of Berne. Perhaps, the name of the club bred a bit of complacency for Spurs were 3-0 down within 28 minutes to a team that treated them as if they were the "young boys". They passed the ball with no little skill and took Spurs apart. A goal just before half time from Bassong gave hope and one from Pavlyuchenko just 7 minutes from the end set up an interesting match for the return. As usual, it would be determined by which particular Spurs' team turned up. Dr Jekyll or Mr Hyde. To the delight of the spectators, for most of the Champions League run, it was to be the former. A return match, 4-0 at home to the Young Boys of Berne, was followed by games against Bremen, Twente, Inter Milan, and AC Milan. Spurs played some wonderfully flowing, attacking football with goals galore before going out to Real Madrid in the quarter final.

To be honest, I hadn't expected them to get as far as they did, so that, when they finally went out, it didn't seem so bad. Failure, maybe, but glorious, wonderful failure that many of those watching will remember for the rest of their lives. Fortunately for me, my son gave me a memory stick for my birthday which I still have somewhere. He had taped the Inter Milan match for me along with the 2-3 away win to Arsenal on 20th November. Spurs had not beaten the arch enemy on their own ground since 1991, 19 long years previously. Biased I may be but the drama that unfolded on that afternoon epitomises what makes a game of football the spectacle that it can be. I may have had heightened emotions which played out in the pub that afternoon. I didn't, however, have great expectations. What unfolded during the next 2 hours encompassed everything that makes us watch the game and reminded me that dreams really can come true, sometimes dramatically so!

If you need reminding, the games started with Sami Nasri refusing to shake hands with William Gallas, a team mate just a few months previously. It must have made the result all the sweeter for the new Spurs man. In the first half Arsenal played as you knew they could. Watching, it felt as though they would score every time they took possession and moved forward. Within 9 minutes Nasri had scored and, 18 minutes later, Charmakh got the second. As the first goal was scored, one of the Arsenal supporters, in jovial mood it must be emphasised, stood up and shouted, "That's the way to do it, that's the way to do it".

God knows how, but Spurs got themselves through to the interval without conceding again. There may still have been hope but you couldn't see where it was coming from other than blind faith. Five minutes after the restart, with Defoe on for Lennon, the former, all five feet six of him, won a header. Van der Vart to Bale and, with the outside of his left foot, he put the ball into the net, 2-1 and game on! A silly handball from Fabregas led to a penalty which van der Vart calmly put away. 23 minutes to play and now game really on. The clincher came from a free kick taken by van der Vart with just four minutes left to play. A glancing header from Younus Kaboul sealed the match and Gallas had the last laugh.

As I left the pub, high as a kite, I sought out the Arsenal fan who had explained to us all how it should be done. As I walked past, I gently tapped him on the shoulder with a smile and the comment, "Now that's how it should be done!" To his great credit, he laughed, replying "You deserved it". Football played at the highest level in a spirit of fierce but friendly rivalry. Just how it should be.

Harry's last season in charge was, for me, a bit of an anti-climax in football terms but dramatic off the field. I think that I had got so used to the team collapsing three quarters of the way through the season that I expected it and wasn't surprised when it happened. Even with the newly acquired Scott Parker, someone I had long thought should have been a Spurs player. Optimistic at one stage that the top three position was the club's to take only for the ten point gap between the club and Arsenal, of all teams, to be closed was frustrating beyond belief. Here we go again. Yet, it had all started so well.

The court case over his tax affairs that had dogged Harry for so long, was coming to a conclusion and the England job, which he had long coveted (how could he not?), was available. The court case won, Spurs went on to thrash Newcastle 5-1 on an afternoon of glorious football. That was in February. Spurs then went on to complete a two month period that included one win, three draws and four defeats, three of them consecutive, amassing a mere 7 points out of a possible 24 to be overtaken with the winning post in sight. The club was then thrashed 5-1 by their other London rivals, Chelsea, in the FA Cup Semi Final. Sixteen days later, Roy Hodgson was appointed as England manager with Harry not even being interviewed. A pity as, in my view, he'd have made a good manager of the national team. Whatever, the euphoria that he must have felt on that sunny February afternoon less than twelve weeks previously, with his financial problems behind him and his team winning in glorious style, must have seemed a distant memory.

Harry, however, hadn't done himself any favours either with some sections of the fans and, presumably, members of the Board. Treating the Europa League with, what appeared to be, disdain cannot have gone down well with the club's hierarchy, flirting with the England job and then, when he was not even interviewed, to say, if press reports are to be believed, that the club needed to get a new contract signed so that they could all plan for the future, wasn't a good move. The news broke on 13 June. The club had parted company with Harry. A dramatic 16 weeks for the club and its supporters reached a climax and with them, the end of the 'Redknapp Years'.

As a fan, I still look back on four seasons of amazing football with fond memories. By any stretch of the imagination, it was a roller coaster of a ride and played havoc with my nervous system. Just what you'd expect as a Spurs' supporter. The next two years saw the appointment of two more managers before the club's fortunes were to change, dramatically.

The Past Few Years

In some ways it's a good thing that I didn't finish this book when I intended to. Life, as usual, in the form of building a new career, got in the way. Allied to, it has to be said, a degree of lackadaisicalness on my part. So, when I last wrote something, a certain Mauricio Roberto Pochettino was the manager at Southampton and Spurs were still only thinking about building a new stadium. Well, what a change has been wrought since May 2014. The world may have continued to turn on its axis and there may have been social and political shocks, the like of which I couldn't have previously imagined. However, events at White Hart Lane have surprised me even more. Not only do Spurs have a new, young manager in the man from Argentina, but he had also changed the culture of the club in a way has even cynical football pundits talking about Spurs as "the best team in the country". Who would have thought it?

In September 2013, the much coveted Gareth Bale left for Real Madrid for a, then, world record fee only, in usual Spurs' fashion, for much of the money to be wasted on the so called "Magnificent 7. These included Paulinho. Chadli, Soldado, Capoue, Chiriches, Lamela and Eriksen. The latter two are the only ones still at the club, of which Eriksen has proven to be a good buy with Lamela being good when he has played but spending half his time out unable to do so.

Cue, eight months later, for Mr Pochettino with his high pressing style of football and his ability to create and mould a team. Moreover, moulding that team, not by buying established stars in the usual Spurs' fashion, but by making players fitter and better than they were. In the process, of course making the total greater than the sum of the individual parts. Those who didn't buy into the double training sessions required for this new level of fitness, or were otherwise judged not to fit the bill, were dispensed with fairly quickly. Planning permission was granted for the new 61,000 seater stadium and, in 2016, work finally started ready, it seems, for the season 2018/9. The latest photos show the scale of this and, it has to be said, it looks impressive.

However it's on the pitch where the real revolution has taken place; created by all that work on the training ground and the further development of a football academy. The latter to help the club nurture and develop young and home grown talent. And, yes, there may be a financial imperative to this, given the comparative wealth of those who own, for example, Chelsea and Manchester City. However, killing two birds with one stone always seems like a good option (if you're into killing birds, that is). So, let's take a look at those past few years.

Well for a start, Bill Nicholson's dictum, "If you have the ball, you're attacking and, if you don't have it, you're defending" is the foundation. Playing football and building from the back. Fast, one touch, accurate football that, at its best is both a pleasure to watch and match winning. League positions of 5th, 3rd and 2nd in the last three seasons with its players winning Young Player of the Year in Harry Kane and Dele Alli (twice). The former also getting the Golden Boot for the last two seasons becoming the first Spurs' player to score more than 20 goals per season, for three seasons, since the fabled J P Greaves. This despite being out injured both last season and the previous one for some weeks. Someone I originally thought was, somewhat, light-weight has proved to be anything but. Proof of this, if nothing else, being his haul of 8 goals in the last two matches of last season, away from home. If you should need reminding, with scores of 1-6 and 1-7! This season, so far, he has been even more impressive.

What is almost as impressive, however, is Spurs' defence and, yes, you heard that right, the defence. Something once, allegedly, described by Bill Shankly as like a pack of cards in its composition. A team whose opposition team talk from Sir Alex Ferguson, was a dismissive, "It's Spurs, lads". Since Mr Pochettino took over, Spurs goals for and against columns have registered, for 2015/5, 58/53, 2015/6, 69/35 and last season, 86/26. And this is Spurs we're talking about! White Hart Lane has become a fortress with the team being unbeaten at home all season. Indeed, their win against Bournemouth was the first time that the team has won 12 consecutive home games since 1919/20. Even I wasn't born then! Still these are just statistics, albeit very good ones, but what about the football?

Well, the players have, obviously, been drilled to within an inch of their lives so that, when it's been good, it's been very good. Slick, accurate, possession football that results in a goal. Indeed, on those occasions, it has often resulted in lots of goals. There are, however, too many times when those in possession seem not to know what to do next; when they look up to see little movement in front of them and opt for passing the ball backwards; this after just running hard and fast to get to where they were, in the first place. Far too many passes across the 18 yard line when something more direct and penetrative is needed. Not enough wing play to the bye line. Far too much reliance on Harry Kane, amazing though he is. It's as if the pressing playing style doesn't allow for any other way and, if that way doesn't work during any match, there is just more of the same. Moreover, the opposition know this.

So, when Spurs make use of their substitutes, these might have fresh legs but they will be fresh legs doing something similar to those who have been substituted. Whereas Chelsea won the recent FA Cup semi final despite being played off the pitch for much of the match. What they did have (and Spurs didn't) were players who are game changers, who did the unexpected. Sometimes it's as if the manager, having been a centre half in his playing days, is less sure in regard to strikers. Money, itself, can hardly be a problem when the club has spent considerable amounts recently on players who haven't made it. Indeed, in one case where most of the football world was surprised at both the player and the amount that is quoted as the fee. He will, undoubtedly, be on his way soon. The question remains, "Why was he bought?"

Now, in case you're thinking that I'm being negative, I'm not. The cultural, practical and, now, physical changes at the club have been remarkable since 2014 and we need to celebrate that and the fact that the future looks brighter than it has since the day I became a supporter, all those years ago.

So let's look at some of those players; players, it has to be said who are the envy of other clubs and who would grace the turf of almost any other in the world. All, also, on long term contacts! Of those who are the first choice plus some of the backup players, there are no real weak links. Other than, of course, one or two expensive buys who don't get much playing time anyway. Yet those latter players and the Chelsea game exposed the lack of depth in a squad that now competes at the top level of English football and plans to go further. That needs to be addressed as it now seems to be happening.

Slow and sure might be the mantra for many businesses; however, it's one that doesn't translate too well to football. Especially if you consider another quote, this one about there being a time and tide in the affairs of men which, taken at the flood, leads onto fortune. With apologies to any women, I would argue that Spurs are now at that point, more so than ever before. So what does that mean in practice? Well, obviously not a change of manager or a strategy that has served them well in recent years. It does, however, require getting rid of some of the players who aren't up to scratch and replacing them with (just a few) who are; notably someone as a back up and to support Harry Kane and another creative midfielder who offers something different in that area. Is there a young Luka Modric out there? So let's look at the players and the future as I would prefer this book to be as much about the latter as the reminiscences of an old man.

The defence speaks for itself; individually and collectively, the best in the Premiership. Loris, despite the odd blip, is a great goalkeeper and just what the team needs in playing from the back. He arrived the complete article and remains so, despite the occasional blip.

As for the full or wing backs, even without Kyle Walker, Spurs have four experienced and quality players and, at least, one youngster with first team experience. Under this manager, Danny Rose has progressed immeasurably and I've always rated Davies and Tripper; the latter of whom especially, can put over a mean cross.

As if the centre back pairing of Vertonghen and Alderwiereld wasn't already the best in the Premiership, the club has dispensed with Kevin Wimmer and brought in a gem in Davinson Sanchez. So make that the best back three in the Premiership. With Eric Dier a capable replacement, dropping back from his defensive midfield duties when necessary. In addition to their defensive duties, Toby certainly makes his presence known in the opposition penalty area and can spray a mean diagonal to the opposite wing. While Mr Vertonghen has recently taken, a la Franz Beckenbauer, to advancing with the ball; in this case, even as far as the opposition's penalty area. Total football here we come.

Eric Dier must have been one of the bargains of the past few years. Indeed, he's already being spoken of as a future Spurs and England captain, although in what position, is unsaid. Able to play at both centre half or defensive midfielder, he seems comfortable in either position. Mind you, he did seem to find the transition from one to the other, earlier in the season, a little difficult, as he tends to when such a change is made during the match. He's still, though, a young player especially as a centre half, a position where experience counts. The fact that Jose Mourinho allegedly wanted him at Manchester United speaks volumes for his potential. Just a little bit of advice if I may, Eric, which

179

manager do you think will help you to develop more as a player?

We now move onto the midfield where Spurs are equally well blessed, both in the offensive and defensive areas. Wanyama is a giant who plays with an upright stance unlike the slightly crouched style of some in his position, for example, Wilson Palacios, of a few years back. Victor strides around his area somewhat imperiously. It's his to own and that he does with a degree of chutzpah and a smile, making sure that the opposition see as little of the ball as possible, let alone actually gain possession of it. The Regimental Sergeant Major of the team.

Next is a player that most supporters recognise for the beast with skill that he is. Able to run directly at the opposition in close control of a ball that seems, at times, to be glued to his feet, Mousa Dembele has come into his own during the past year or so. As strong as an ox, it is nigh on impossible to get the ball off him when he's on one of his runs. The last time I saw a Spurs player with such strength, power and close control may have been watching Martin Chivers. Yet I feel that, with Mr Dembele, there is more to come as long as his continuing foot problem can be dealt with.

A player, however, who I feel could do even more for the club is Christian Eriksen. Indeed, his recent performance for his country, including a hat trick, demonstrated just how much more he's capable of. Spurs need that extra and to do whatever is necessary to ensure that he's able to give it that so that the club can step up to the next level. His free kicks are always likely to bear fruit as are his crosses from deep. Note the latter that, recently, brought three goals against Chelsea; usually a team whose players take great personal offense to the opposition scoring. Without any disrespect for what he does for the team, more of this, please.

We now move on to a player who seems to have the world at his feet (and his head, given the aforementioned Eriksen's crosses). Ladies and gentlemen, I give you Deli Alli. Skill, ability and with no little determination not to be pushed around by those with more experience, he has all the makings of a complete midfielder. Yes he can be impetuous and act like a young boy at times but if he curbs that behavior, he can be a football legend in the manner of Steven Gerard, Frank Lampard and David Beckham. Indeed, he had already scored more goals (40) than those three combined at a similar age (21). The world, as they say, is his oyster so let's hope that he spends his career at Spurs.

We now move on to another player who frustrated me last year but who went on to enjoy a purple patch in front of goal. Heung Min Son (Sonny to supporters). Still prone to not seeing when someone is in a better position, he has a striker's eye for goal. He is also extremely hard working and, his perception of his team mates' positions notwithstanding, is a real team player. Another one who plays with a smile in his face. Long may it continue.

Lastly, someone who it took me sometime to realise really has it all as a striker. Please stand up Mr Harry Kane. My perception of him was, partly, fuelled by my experience of Spurs' home grown strikers going back over 50 years. How could this one be any different? After all he was no Didier Drogba or Romelu Lukaku in his build. Well, I was wrong, he has strength in abundance, along with no little skill and, it would seem, a determination that has to be seen. Lastly, he works his socks off for the team. My apologies, Harry. My bitter experience has been confounded by someone from much younger generation who doesn't have that baggage. If newspaper reports, that you see your long term future at Spurs, are to be believed, you really will be a legend.

So, moving on to those who are (or were) next in line, among whom is one Vincent Jannsen. Now, I have to confess that, like most other supporters, I desperately wanted him to succeed. He worked hard for the team and certainly put in the effort. So, what went wrong? Well whatever it was, so far, it shows little sign of getting much better in Turkey. That would be a pity for him, both personally and professionally. Interestingly, he follows two other Spurs' strikers whose time at the club didn't go as well as expected, namely Roberto Soldado and Sergei Rebrov, who also finished up at Fenerbahce. It also leads to questions being raised about the club's record of acquisitions to fill this position over a period of some years. Answers to this, please, on a postcard to whoever is responsible.

Which leads me onto a broader point which is that Spurs have needed a back up striker for virtually the whole of the time that Mauricio Pochettino has been the manager and haven't solved an acknowledged problem. Three years ago, he inherited Adebeyor, Soldado and a very young Harry Kane. In the first year the first of these departed and in the second, so did the second. Sonny is good but not a direct replacement so now we have Fernando Llorente. I know that it's still early days, however, he too seems not to be finding the back of the net as often as often as might have been expected when he was bought. Nor is he getting much time on the pitch. All of which leads me to think that there is a problem of some sort in finding that back up player for the inestimable Mr Kane.

You could argue that, despite been sidelined by injuries during the last two seasons, we have managed well with that strategy. However, you could just as well argue that, if we'd had someone of equal stature to take his place, we might have put in an even greater challenge in each of those seasons. That's certainly a view that I would agree with. And, yes, I know that you build a team from the back, as Spurs have done. After all, if you don't concede a goal, you won't lose. At which point, I would quote the club motto to you and say, "Please, Mr Levy, buy another top quality striker, as well as another playmaker".

The team will then be complete and able to compete with Chelsea and Manchester City despite the vast difference in spending power. Given that Spurs have the youngest average age in their squad in the Premiership, that team will have some years to develop even further and, with its new stadium, who knows what it will achieve? The future's bright and it's white (with blue shorts).

Energia Universal

So how has Mr Pochettino worked his magic on a club that, with the occasional good season, has underperformed for many years? Now that's any easy one to answer. He's changed the psychology and whole culture at the club. Now, that wasn't difficult was it? Well, as someone who's rescued a number of charities from closure, albeit organisations on a considerably smaller scale, I do have some experience of this situation. Crucial to such success are a clear vision and strategy, no little determination and, crucially, the support of those employing you; the latter not always too evident in professional football, especially in the upper echelons. And even more so these days. Yet the manager has done it, so much so that, in his three years at the club, the team has finished 5th, 3rd and 2nd. Furthermore, even this long term supporter is optimistic for the future! And for someone who follows Spurs, that's saying something.

Not only that but that he has done this without the usual Spurs' reliance on readymade stars. Indeed, he has disposed of a number of these since he joined. So much so that, of the 18 man match day squad that featured when they went to Villa Park in November 2014 with a record of 3 wins, 4 defeats and 2 losses, only 8 are still at the club. After being one goal down at half time, they went on to win 2-1 in a match that the manager regarded as a turning point. It may not be a coincidence that Harry Kane replaced Adebayor in that match and scored the winner with a deflected free kick in stoppage time.

So, what's behind the turnaround? Well according to a recent article in *The Observer* by David Hytner, it's "Energia Universal"; a concept that has shaped Mauricio Pochettino's life and informs his footballing philosophy. According to the article, the best way to describe it is as a life force that influences everything; that everything is connected and nothing happens without cause but, rather, as a consequence of something else. This seems a perfect fit for football and explains the manager's attention to detail and the way that he handles the players.

Now, as a long established supporter I very much wanted them to win everything but accepted that they wouldn't. Instead, I settled for a Harry Redknapp style of play. Even if they came up short, it was exciting to watch and helped me to believe. The result is that it has taken me a while to warm to this manager's style. Indeed, even now, as I've said, I find the passing back to be a little too much, as I do with the continual sideways passing across the 18 yard line; so much so that I want to shout, "For god's sake, have a bloody shot". And, yes, I do know that winning football is dependent on possession but a little more flowing movement would help. Then I remember that radical change that has taken place at the club and I keep the faith. So much so that it's hard not to believe that, within the next few seasons, the club will win something major. The new stadium, of course, also being a requirement for entry into the big league. It is, of course, bigger then Arsenal's!

On his arrival, Pochettino made it his mission to toughen the mentality of the team and no one could argue that he hasn't succeeded in that task. This was important, both of itself and because he believes that everything is related to energy and the high pressing style of play that he demands. In pursuit of this, pre-season training sessions are remorseless, in order that the players are able and ready to fight to the very end of the game. Indeed, their ability to run during the last minute as they did in the first, is a notable facet of their play.

In a way in which modern rugby players are fast, mobile and with a physique intended to intimidate weaker opposition, this breed of Spurs' player has a similar stamp. Hence, it takes a specific type of player to buy into this ethos and meet these demands and it didn't need a genius to see who didn't. So he began by giving the more senior players the opportunity to show what they could do; reasoning, it would seem that, if he had thrown the youngsters in at the deep end and the experiment had failed, it would then have been difficult to reverse the process. However, it should have been clear from his work at Southampton, that he preferred to work with younger players who he could mould and develop; those who were tactically flexible, who were physically imposing, full of desire, open to fresh ideas and of a certain character. In return, he allows them an element of freedom and treats them as individuals. It helps, of course that, at 45, he is young enough to be matey with his players but old enough to have their respect.

Spurs, for example, don't have a code of conduct that players are expected to sign up to; the latter aren't fined for being a few minutes late for training. What is actually important is that principles need to be respected as, above all, must be the manager. Given his track record and what he is now creating at Spurs, this shouldn't be too difficult. So how does this translate in practice?

Well, for someone steeped in the old ways of the club, it really has been a sea change. It's no longer about building a team by buying established stars with the emphasis on attack; where, if you gave a goal away, you just went to the other end and scored again. Where flair was our watchword and what sustained the supporters when the team played with that quality but failed to win. Danny Blanchflower's dictum was ingrained in our DNA. Indeed, it was why we supported the club in the first place. Don't get me wrong, we wanted the team to win but it had to be with a certain style, a certain élan. After all, it's "Audere est Facere" isn't it?

Well the world has moved on and during that time the club has slipped down the financial pecking order. Moreover, it now has an expensive new stadium under construction and needs to operate in a different way. Enter Mr Pochettino.

In this new model, young, preferably home grown, players are nurtured and, developed with those who make the grade, tied into long term contracts. Those who don't are sold to clubs lower in the league for a commendable profit. I suspect that Mr Levy is delighted with this. Moreover, it's paying dividends. To quote the manager, Spurs "is a completely different project to the big sides". Indeed, it wouldn't be difficult to make the argument that they are creating a template for the other Premiership clubs to follow. Except, of course, the usual suspects of both Manchester teams and Chelsea.

In terms of the team, Pochettino is sensitive to "negative personal energy" and makes sure that he knows everything about each individual player; how they feel, how they react. He talks of "putting our energy" into a particular player while "giving our love" to another one. Faith and belief in what you can do are important as is the need to feel those emotions. In this way, he puts that feeling into individuals and gives them confidence. Not for him the public demeaning of his players.

This is demonstrated with those who, for example, have little chance at present of displacing, say, Hugo Loris. They are talked up because they, too, need to feel that positive energy. They have to be primed and ready when they are needed, as members of the same football family, as everyone else. In this way, he knows that a replacement is always tuned in and ready to play. It's why he seldom, if ever, complains about injuries and has confidence in the team. Consider how they maintained their momentum last season despite injuries, sometimes longer term, to key players; notably Alderweireld, Dembele, Kane, Lamela, Lloris, Rose and Vertonghen.

To the manager, every member of the squad is an individual whose psyche needs to be understood in order to get the best out of each of them. This psychological approach, allied to the way that the staff use data to analyse performance is said to be extraordinary in its detail. In this way, the club is able to devise bespoke programmes for its players. So much so that there have been occasions when there are eight different types of training in one day. The manager knows when a player needs to train or rest, when they need a carrot or a stick. Over its record run of winning games last season, he has pushed the team rather than relaxed them on the basis that players with their tails up are more receptive.

As a result, the improvement in many players has been pronounced; Danny Rose being a notable example. The club is certainly on the up in a solid way that it hasn't been during much of the time that I've supported it. If it continues in this way, trophies will be a natural consequence. On which positive note and in keeping with the manager's philosophy, I'd like to reiterate that I support a team that, in footballing terms at least, represents a positive view of the world, a style and a culture that I adhere to; one in which the ends do not justify the means. Which leads me, nicely, to the future.

What Does the Future Hold?

Well, even for a lifetime Spurs' supporter, the future looks good; in fact, as I've already written, probably better than at any other time that I've watched the team play. If you add in the new stadium, you really do have all the ingredients for success; however, this is Spurs' that we're talking about. So, is this new dawn different? Well I think that it is for a number of reasons.

The first of these the club has, by accident or design, managed to appoint a manager who arrived with a clear vision of the type of football that he wanted the team to play and, after 3 years, is still backing him. Furthermore, given the cultural change that he's brought to the club and his record on the pitch to date, there is little sign of that backing being withdrawn. In addition, the playing style that he utilises is best brought to fruition with young players who buy into it and not established and older stars. The fact that the former are likely to be considerably cheaper than the latter is a bonus. Finally, and as I've mentioned previously, those players who prove not to make the required grade can then be sold at a very reasonable profit. The whole set up a better and more sustainable financial template, especially for a club with a stadium to pay for. Moreover, in terms of its football and its finance, it is one that other clubs are taking note of. What's not to like? Well, again, as I've already remarked, the football can be less flowing and a little more hesitant and cautious than this traditional supporter prefers. I suspect that Mr Pochettino is well aware of this.

So, for the first time in my memory, it looks as though the sum of the individual parts at the club are greater as a team. Too often in the past the opposite has been the case. The downside, about which it's too early to judge, could be that the level of fitness and commitment required for the style of play, may mean that players are only able to sustain this for fewer seasons. This, itself, may lead to a greater turnover of those players. We'll just have to wait and see. In the meantime, it's as good a time to be a Spur's supporter as I can remember and that's no bad thing. Optimism, in these trying times being something that we could all do with more of.

As for the immediate future, well second in the premiership is better than I'd expected at the beginning of the last season and Dele Alli has been a revelation. Mind you, if our track record in the matches that we've played at Wembley recently is any guide, we may have a few hiccoughs along the way. We may also, if Professor Wenger is any guide, have some acclimatising to deal with in the new stadium. However, 2018 and beyond offer real grounds for optimism. Once again, the future's bright and it's lilywhite. However, I am a Spurs' supporter so perhaps it's best to keep one's fingers crossed, just in case.

So Why Don't I Just Support Arsenal?

Simply because I support Tottenham. In truth, I could no more transfer my allegiance to another club than I could change my skin. It's an inherent part of me, as natural as the sun coming up in the morning and going down in the evening. Admittedly, for years now I have been an armchair supporter but a supporter nonetheless. I am less irrational and more objective about the club that I was in the past as I hope this book demonstrates. Yet I am still Tottenham through and through. A rational person, I cannot rationalise it and that irrationality has passed onto my son who is now in his 50's. When he visits from Yorkshire, we still, very occasionally, go to a game but the intensity of the mania that I had isn't there. It's not the game it's me as I certainly make a great deal of noise in our local when I'm watching footie. I think that, in the past, going to the ground and watching was more participatory whereas, now, it's less so.

I am now a spectator watching a game of football from what I expect to be comfortable surroundings. The pub, combined with the close up detail and overview that you get on television, is something I am not prepared to be without.

A shame really but that sense of spectacle and occasion is not there quite as it was. Part of it is age; when I was younger, I didn't mind standing for hours, sometimes in the rain and cold, just to watch a match. Nowadays, I want comfort and a great view. Important though the occasion is, the former now overrides the latter. Such are the vicissitudes of age.

Anyway, does anyone know of someone who has changed their footballing allegiance? I certainly don't although I have heard, on some of the phone in programmes, of people who support more than one club. It's a concept I and millions of others don't understand. But then again, I don't understand Jane Austen. Reading the minutiae of the lives of well to do people in the 19th Century has never seemed to me to be a congenial leisure pursuit but, each to their own. Now reading, "The Ragged Trousered Philanthropist" was a very useful and enjoyable exercise which only goes to show which side of the political divide I come down on. Anyway, back to football.

Support for a club is acquired, sometimes inherited but not inherent. Once acquired, though, it seems to become a way of life that gets hardwired in. It's not even that you can switch off and ignore it. It is an allegiance that, once so acquired, is forged. It can't really be changed. The players change and most of them don't support the club they play for. Harry Redknapp I understand, for example, was an Arsenal supporter as a kid and presumably still is. Yet he would celebrate with the best of them when he was the Spurs' manager. The manager and other staff change, the owners change, the ground even moves and, occasionally, the name changes as well, like Wimbledon to MK Dons; in the latter case, both at the same time. The fans, though, through thick and thin, good times and bad remain loyal. They cannot do other. My own view, for what it's worth is that those circumstances are about as likely as, to quote someone in regard to winning the lottery, of finding Elvis alive on the moon.

So, why not Arsenal? Well, as I've tried to explain so far, it's now hardwired in, something that those who don't support a team of some sort won't understand. Yet I feel the need for such an explanation. Yes, Arsenal, during the Professor's time, have played some wonderful, purist football. They have won honours in the relatively recent past, including going a whole season without being defeated, a remarkable achievement. They also have a 60,000 seat stadium within a mile of the posher parts of Islington. Despite the fact that he professes no other interests than football and dedicates his life to it, the Professor appears to be an academic among managers. The trouble is now that even his time may be up within the next few years. Ironically just as, after over 20 years of living in their shadow, their deadly rivals are on their way up. They've completed Mauricio's third season in charge by finishing as runners up and bettering the previous two seasons' positions and their goals for and against columns. Moreover the new stadium is under construction with plans for it to be ready for the season after next. This, when built, will be the biggest in London. Like I said, the future looks bright

So, with all my irrationality, I will continue my allegiance waiting for the day when Spurs, once again, sit at the top of the Premiership at the end of the season and go on to win the Champions League again and again. Is it likely? Well it can happen, something even I am getting my head around. In the meantime, I can dream, can't I? It's what I and many other Spurs' supporters have been doing for years and, I suspect, it's what sustains us; the hope. As I tried to explain to my wife, I can't "just support Arsenal".

PS. 10 November 2017, Eric Dier captains England.

References and Sources

"*Broken Dreams*" by Tom Bower

"*Living on the Volcano*" by Michael Galvin

"*I am the Secret Footballer*"

"*Mr Moon Has Left the Stadium*" by Jeremy Nicholas

"*A Romance of Football, the History of Tottenham Hotspur Football Club 1892 – 1921*" reprinted by The Tottenham and Edmonton Weekly Herald

David Hytner article in The Guardian

Barney Ronay article in The Guardian

22349802R00115

Printed in Poland
by Amazon Fulfillment
Poland Sp. z o.o., Wrocław